I0024301

Cuming Hall

The Power of an Endless Life

Cuming Hall

The Power of an Endless Life

ISBN/EAN: 9783337813482

Printed in Europe, USA, Canada, Australia, Japan

Cover: Foto ©Thomas Meinert / pixelio.de

More available books at **www.hansebooks.com**

THE POWER

OF

AN ENDLESS LIFE

BY

THOMAS C. HALL

PASTOR OF THE FOURTH PRESBYTERIAN CHURCH,
CHICAGO

CHICAGO
A. C. McCLURG AND COMPANY
1894

COPYRIGHT
BY A. C. McCLURG AND CO.
A. D. 1894

PREFACE.

ONLY the kind insistence of friends, and
more particularly of one friend, whose judgment I have learnt more and more to trust,
and to whom I desire to dedicate this little
volume, leads me to add to the many books
that clamor for our time. Without any thought
of more than a possible and passing interest
in the form of the message, it is the earnest
hope that some may find in these pages a word
to their deepest life. The form is that of the
direct appeal. Repetitions mark the frag-
mentary character of the preparation, but the
sermons were written with the profound con-
viction that more deeply than ever must organized Christianity enter into the secrets of our
Lord and King, and learn from Christ "The
Power of an Endless Life."

T. C. H.

CONTENTS.

THE

POWER OF AN ENDLESS LIFE.

———◆———

I.

FORMS OF GODLINESS.

*Holding a form of godliness, but having denied
the power thereof: from these also turn away.*
—2 TIM. iii. 5.

THIS warning is interesting as an in-
dication of what Paul already saw
coming into the life of the ancient primitive church. Some would persuade us
that the church of the first three centuries
was a model church in every way, but
even during the life of Paul very nearly
all the marks of degradation and disinte-
gration that are to be seen more clearly
working later on were already before his
prophetic eye. Indeed, before three cen-

turies had passed the church had corrupted herself alike in doctrine and in ritual.

It is also interesting to see that Paul here makes the sharp distinction which later philosophy has emphasized and developed, the distinction between the form and the essential, between expression and power, between accident and that which is real. This distinction has passed into the thinking of the present generation more particularly through the transcendental philosophy of Germany, so that it is a commonplace, familiar thing with us, many of us dwelling upon it without knowing very clearly the origin of the idea.

It is perfectly clear to any one that reflects, that the form and the essence are not the same, that the essence is something so intangible that it is often very difficult to describe. But no matter how imperfect the form, the essential under-

neath the form is after all the real thing,
the other is accidental. The forms in
which men hold godliness are of infinite
variety. What is godliness? Godliness is just what the word tells you; it
is *god-li-ness*, or the quality of being like
God. In Him we live, and move, and
have our being. The old Greek poet
saw that clearly, and Paul emphasizes
his statement and endorses it by quoting
him. We feel in our better moments
how helpless we are to do right, and in
our better moments we attribute all our
right doing to the divine impulse that
is in our life. This is the real spiritual
meaning of the doctrine of total corruption. It is the expression of the
sense within us that we are helpless
apart from God, that it is only as
God lives in us that righteousness is
godliness. Wherever, therefore, we find
anything that is admirable, it has its
source in the divine, God is to have the

glory. This is the real foundation of
the hope that is strong in every one of
us, that Christ is much larger than the
historic knowledge of Christ; that wherever there is self-sacrifice, wherever there
is hungering of the soul for God, wherever there is the breaking, contrite heart,
there is the revelation of the presence of
God. The Christ as manifested in the
historical form is the incarnation of that
complete godliness, the other forms of
which, so far as they are human, are
always more or less imperfect.

So you will see also that there are
forms of godliness so incomplete that
they are masked caricatures of the Christ-
like life. Indeed, if you thoughtfully consider the familiar forms of godliness, you
will find in them all some element of the
caricature that men are so apt to trace
in the lines of the picture. The pagan
forms of godliness seem at first sight
warped out of all semblance to religious

life ; loaded down with iniquity, heartless selfishness, gross sensuality. Heathen worship, so far as it has value, has it only as an imperfect expression of the craving of the human heart to come to that divine source of which every man at some time in his life feels a longing to drink. But all worship has value as by it we find ourselves in contact with God. This contact is divine life, however much we may caricature it, however poor the expression we may give it, however rude may be our conception of what the reality is.

In history we see jostling each other forms of godliness, such as the philosophy of heathendom contrasted with primitive Christianity, as paganism was contrasted with Judaism. The forms of godliness as we see them in pagan Greece and pagan Rome, were such as indicate that philosophy represented an advance on the popular forms of Roman and Greek godliness. Hence philosophy set to work to destroy these older forms, but its weakness was that it put in their place a form only a little better.

Then there are the forms of godliness which we see in the splendid basilicas and glorious cathedrals and the monasteries of the Middle Ages, — forms of godliness splendid in their outward appearance, high, imposing, majestic to the imaginations of men; forms under which the deep underlying craving of the human heart for some expression of divinity sought to make itself felt in the world's real history. There are the forms of godliness as we find them in the theological scholasticism of the seventeenth century, — the scholasticism which, just as the primitive Christianity undermined the Jewish philosophy, sought in its turn to undermine the forms of godliness under which the religious spirit had expressed itself for fifteen centuries, because it had found, and knew in its heart of hearts, that these forms were interfering with the growth of the divine life in its fuller expression. Scholasticism was also only a form, and it had to give way to some-thing better. The Evangelical Emotion-alism was a form under which a better godliness, a new appreciation of the Christ life, a holier conception of what life ought to be, sought to undermine scholastic mediævalism that Christ might be still more plainly seen.

Now can any nineteenth-century com-munity, I might almost say any nine-teenth-century congregation, say that all these forms of godliness are not more or less expressed among us? There is dog-matism among us, plenty of it, undiluted, most undisguised dogmatism. There is heathenism among us, heathenism that voices itself precisely in the sceptical, cynical, sneering philosophy which was on the lips of Cæsar and Cicero. There

is among us the baptized dogmatism that
formed the life of the church of the third
and tenth centuries, — a baptized dogmatism whose whole conception is æsthetic,
and which is satisfied with the husks of
externalism without coming in contact
with the reality.   There is mediæval scholasticism among us.   It is found most
largely expressing itself from the pulpit,
but there is plenty of it there.   There is
evangelicalism in all its strength, in all its
weakness among us.   Sometimes it is not
power, sometimes it is a form of godliness that is made up of a great many
forms; it is the synthesis, the putting
together of many forms; it is the corruption of the divine idea.   We are, to-day
as ever, in danger of holding the forms
of godliness without the power thereof.

    You may ask, then, is it a matter of
indifference whether we are pagans or
heathens;   whether we   hold   mediæval
scholasticism,   or   evangelical   forms?

Yes, it may be a matter of complete indifference. If you are denying the power,
you might as well deny the power under
one form as another. If you are denying
the power of God, it is all one to High
Heaven under what form you make your
denial. In the last days there shall come
those who shall hold the forms of godliness, but deny the power thereof.

What is the power of godliness? The
New Testament is so full of it that we
have not seen it. It forms so much of
Paul's writings that we have almost entirely ignored it. It is so important a
factor that we have left it out. It is of
so real moment in our religious life that
we have let it pass us. The power of
God is the divine indwelling promised
when the Holy Spirit came down at
Pentecost, promised to every man who
will share with the early disciples the
Pentecostal moment. It is God in us.
It is the Holy Spirit speaking to and

inspiring us in the inspired book, or in
the church, or in the pulpit, — inspiring
us to right doing, to right living, to right
thinking, to right sacrifice.

This is the power of godliness; and
our denials of it, however much we may
cover them in words, amount always to
the same thing. We deny it in a hundred ways. We say to ourselves that our
form is convenient, that we are satisfied
with the present. The power of godliness denied in the interests of the form
is the real weakness of the individual,
the social, the Christian life. Let us see
what is the power of this godliness. It
is the power of God. What did it do in
New Testament times? It shook men
so that with blanched faces they saw the
coming judgment, so that with trembling
voices they declared to their generation
what were the penalties of unrighteousness. It shook men so that their lives
were changed. They forgot the past

and flung themselves into the future,
careless of what it brought forth for them.
The power of godliness made them new
men in Christ Jesus, sent them to the
cross if need were, that men might know
that the power of God was righteousness
and righteousness altogether, and that
denial was death.

There was seen the power of that godliness when about the tenth century men
began to realize that things could not go
on as they were going. The monasteries
were heaps of corruption. The priests
were blind leaders of the blind. The
nobles had added field to field and house
to house until there was no place for the
starving peasant, who had to accept anything the insolent nobles chose to give
them. These warred among themselves
until blood covered all the hills; but if the
peasant dared lift his hand they would
stop their wars among themselves and
unite in still further trampling upon the

neck of the down-trodden serf, grinding
him into the dust, mingling his blood
with their sacrifices and his flesh with
their feasts. Things could not go on as
as they were. The power of godliness
seized on one or two men, and they went
forth with voices shaken with the thun-
ders of Sinai and melting with the mercy
of the Mount, telling men that the King
would come, and that their judgment
was of heaven. Men did repent for a
little. God did lift for a little the clouds
that hung over them. Yet they again
forgot him. Then he baptized Europe
in blood. Europe deserved it: and
out of her ruins he fenced a new vine-
yard, and built a new wine-press, and he
looks for grapes: it is for you and me to
say what he will find. Will he find
grapes, or only wild grapes?

The power of godliness was displayed
in a very startling way in two countries
very near to each other; and we have a

prophetic voice telling us in accents that
ought to ring down the ages what came
of the power of godliness denied in
France. Read Carlyle's History of the
French Revolution, and learn what the
power of godliness denied brought forth.
Over England hung precisely the same
prophetic clouds. The conditions in
England, if we are to trust the historian,
were not very much better than the conditions in France; but the power of godliness became manifest, and changed the
lives of two Oxford students, who gathered a few more students around them.
The power of godliness shook them, and
they went down to the Cornish miners.
They gathered these miners about them ;
the tears rolled down their faces, these
poor, despised, outcast members of society! There were Pentecostal waves
which shook England from centre to
centre, rolled over into this country where
conditions were becoming very bad in-

deed, and they stopped for a little the
processes that were going on here with
such frightful rapidity. The power of
godliness saved England for a little.

Now the power of godliness is a very
strange thing. All power is. You cannot put your finger upon it. If I were
to speak to you about the power of
gravitation, you might know its laws, you
might know its results. You might say
that it shows itself so and so, and in-
creases in such and such a ratio ; that it
holds the world together in such and
such a way. But what is gravitation?
You do not know, nor does any one. The
best explanation that is given of it en-
counters so many insuperable mathemati-
cal objections that there is practically no
adequate explanation of what gravitation
is. The power that makes our spring
creep slowly upon us, — the power of the
sun's heat, — we know not either what it
is. We can change the heat into light,

and the motion into electricity; we can change the electricity into lifting power; we can even take the electricity and in some mysterious way change it into vital power, and putting it through the roots of trees and plants greatly increase their vital activity. There is some strange correlation of all the physical powers round about us; but if you were to ask scientific men what is the power, they would say they do not know; they only know its results, and that is all science deals with.

Now we know the power of godliness only as we see it exemplified in results. You see the little bud in its hard case. If the hail were to come it would only jump off the hard enclosed bud; but the power of the sun is going to break through that hard case, and the little bud will fling itself out into God's sunshine with all the laughter of new green leaves to hail the joy of the coming summer.   The denial of the power of godliness is the denial of that which can change the forms of life as they are about us.   If you say, " I do not believe in the power of the spring: I do not believe in this power of the sun; I do not believe what you tell me of the strange alchemy of the chemists; " I can only take you out and show you the bud bursting into the fulness of its joy, and say,   "Something did that; some power there was that did that.   I cannot analyze it for you, but it is there."   The form is nothing; if the power is there it will make its own form, it will find its own expression.   The denial of the power of godliness is the denial that there is in this world a divine life capable of changing the human heart, breaking its hardness, changing the stony heart into a heart of flesh, making us sympathetic, tender, and true. The denial of the power of godliness is the denial of the power to do this thing.

That denial is written large in the lives
of some of us, though we hold the forms
of godliness. You say, " I am sound in
in my orthodoxy, I accept the Shorter
Catechism and the Confession of Faith ;
I believe everything." And what does it
amount to? It may amount to this, that
you are holding the forms of godliness;
and the servant in your household, the
employee in your office, the tenant in
your dwelling, and the dependent upon
you or the employer who is over you,
looks for the true power, and sees rather
the awful denial of the power of godliness, making you selfish, making you
unlovable, making you a lover of pleas-
ure and not a lover of God, denying in
your lives the things you profess in the
church ; so that men and women who
know religion only as you have taught
it to them, say that it is hard and cold,
a dreary, barren intellectual belief, a
dogma, and they cannot accept it, and say,

"Away with it!" They learn from you
to deny, not the power, that they never
see, but the form of godliness, and then
you weep over their scepticism. You
have friends, you have wives, you have
husbands, you have dependents, you have
employers; how is it? Are the forms of
godliness that you practise so full of
power that they are the natural expression of the divine life written on your
very brow? as when Stephen stood up
before those who denied the power of
godliness, and as he looked his face
became as the face of an angel, telling
them to their faces of their sin, rehears-
ing all the ills, all the vices, all the iniquity of the past history of the children
of Israel till at last they could stand it
no longer, and they gnashed their teeth
at him and took him and stoned him.
"Jerusalem! Jerusalem! thou that ston-
est the prophets and slayest those that
are sent unto thee, how often would I

have gathered thy children together, even as a hen gathereth her chickens under her wings, and ye would not."

We come out from morning to morning to God's house. We sing hosannas to Jesus Christ. We claim him as Master. We entreat him to be with us. We hold the forms of godliness; but, let us ask ourselves, are we holding the forms of godliness and denying the power thereof? If it is so, that is the only infidelity that will really wreck the world. The infidelity that points out the mistakes of Moses from the public platform will do no harm if only, being faithful and not denying the power of godliness, you do not give wings to every shaft of infidelity. If only you lift up the cross in a life of self-denial and self-sacrifice, if only you live so that the world will take knowledge of you that you have been with Jesus, if only Christ is in your life, you need have no fear of infidelity, no

fear for the world. It is God's world, and
he will reign in it, even if he turn and
overturn until our present industrial sit-
uation, our organized Christianity, our
political institutions are broken if need
be into the trodden dust of the ages, and
there come a new heaven and a new
earth wherein dwelleth righteousness,
and Christ is King forever and ever.

II.

THE POWER OF AN ENDLESS LIFE.

And what we say is yet more abundantly evident, if after the likeness of Melchizedek there ariseth another priest, who hath been made, not after the law of a carnal commandment, but after the power of an endless life. — HEB. vii. 15 – 16.

THIS chapter is not strictly an argument in the sense in which we shall find that word used in our books of formal logic. It is rather a forcible illustration. It is from the story of Melchizedek, with which the Jewish imagination had dealt rather liberally. As all easily recall the details of that story, it is unnecessary to dwell upon the various conceptions that grew up in the later Jewish history around this symbolic figure. Melchizedek greets Abraham. Abraham acknowledges him as priest

and king, and pays him tithes for some
reason that is unknown to us. That he
was a worshipper of the same God that
Abraham acknowledged, that Abraham
in some way or other was desirous of
acknowledging either his moral or religious supremacy, is undoubted. Beyond
that it is not useful for us to go. As an
illustration this story has great weight,
for the writer to the Hebrews has explained at considerable length to those
to whom he was writing that the Jewish
religion had not passed away, that they
did not of necessity break with the national Judaism when they accepted Christianity. All that had passed away was
the form, and that had absolutely passed
away. Now there was a better revelation, — not a new revelation, but a better
and higher revelation of that very thing
toward which Judaism had been only
pointing. The argument of the book
centres around that one thought. The

writer also points out that the real priesthood was not bound up with lineal
descent; that the priesthood existed inde-
pendently of the forms of Judaism; that
such a priesthood, whatever its change
in character, was ever the same in its
essential religious meaning, — that it
was in fact the priesthood established in
Christ, who, he says, is a priest after the
order of Melchizedek.

Now what distinguishes this non-
Judaic priesthood? It was the isolated
character of Melchizedek in bold antithesis to the Jewish priestly family; and
it is to this antithesis between the real
and the symbolic, between the temporal
and the eternal, that the author directs
our attention. Christ is claimed as priest,
not of law, but of power; not of carnal
commandment, but after the power of an
endless life. Here there are contrasts,
— law as over against power, law being
only the expression, in many cases indeed

only the temporary expression of power.
Power must be behind law. The law
may change. Indeed, because power
only can last, therefore the law must
change. This is a fact familiar to every
historical jurist.

And not after a carnal commandment
is Christ a priest, — a carnal commandment having to do simply with circumstances which are temporal and changing, —
but after the power of an indissoluble life.
This is the uniqueness that is claimed for
Christ, that he is the power that passeth
not away, — " Jesus Christ, the same yesterday, to-day and forever," a priest not
after a carnal commandment, not after
law, but after the power of an endless
life. I believe if we could only fix that
contrast in our minds it would give us
light upon some of the things that puzzle
and perplex us. We should sometimes
fail indeed to separate between the temporal and eternal elements, but we should

not be discouraged because we thus failed. There are some marked phenomena of life that might be more easily explained to us if we would remember this contrast between power and the expression of it. Take for instance the religions, even those which are beyond the pale of the immediate revelation granted to us in Christ. Surely there we may see something of this power which cannot be identified with the forms which we have come to recognize as weak, imperfect, and temporary. Of course, I cannot speak of the natural religions from the standpoint of one that knows them thoroughly; I can only take the testimony of those who are competent to judge, as I am not. Take, for instance, the testimony concerning Buddhism. It is useless for us to deny the power that Buddhism has had over men's lives. It started very much as Protestantism started, as a reaction against the formal-

ity and corruption of the older Brahmanism. Buddhism started as a reform,
with no intention of breaking away from
Brahmanism, with no intention of doing
more than instilling into the older religion a force and vitality which it was
only too evident it had lost. Now, the
forms in which Buddhism comes to us
are most evidently immaterial. Its philosophy has changed so completely that
the schools of Buddhism are as numerous
as the schools of Protestantism. All that
is outward finds the greatest variety
exhibited in its development. It is, of
course, an easy explanation of its power
to say that it was born of the devil; that
was the older Christian explanation, but
the ideas and spirit of the New Testament teach us to understand more prop-
erly the influence it has had over men's
lives. Certainly its power was not in
that it was a popular proclamation. It
was not a mystic dream. Its power was

not in pandering to men's appetites. It preached sternly at all times upon a very high and noble level the doctrine of self-sacrifice and self-abnegation. Nor did it hold out certain popular dreams, certain hopes that men would readily grasp after. It did nothing of the kind. It never tempted men with dreams of a paradise in exchange for the life here. Its insistence was upon a life of righteousness here and now, and it held out as almost the only hope for the future an escape from the evils incident to the life that is now.

Take, on the other hand, the religion of Mohammed. Again we see that there is something that must be deeper than the forms of Mohammedanism, for these forms we have come to recognize as weak and imperfect. Now it is a very easy explanation of Mohammedanism to say that it was advanced by the power of the sword. But did you ever know of another instance where a nation of drunk-

ards and gamblers was made moral by
any temporal power? If so, I wish very
much that Mohammed's sword could be
unsheathed in America. It is a very easy
explanation of the power of Mohammedanism to say that it was the genius of
one man. If that is true, how is it to be
explained that the genius of Mohammed
gave birth to a long succession of men of
genius, on the very lines of Mohammed's
power, that, for instance, it should pro-
duce a Saladin, who showed himself a
nobler man than most of his Christian
opponents? It is a comparatively easy
explanation to say that the wild hopes
of a temporal paradise tempted men to
be moral. The experience of human life
is that men are not tempted to morality
by any such means. We must recognize,
if we are honest, that behind all that is
temporary and weak and imperfect in
Judaism, in Mohammedanism, in Buddhism, in any of the religions whose

forms we have come to recognize as in-
efficient, there is something that needs to
be revealed more perfectly, to be known
and grasped at fully, if we would have
the explanation of the religious life, and
the power of that religious life over the
characters and hopes of men.

We see in church history something
of the dangers of forgetting the human
character of Christ Jesus our Lord.   We
see some of the perils that come from a
too sharp separation of his humanity from
our humanity.   Nothing could be more
profitable for us than to dwell from time
to time, with anxious thought for God's
blessing as we do so, upon what is the
real power of Christ's life as he presents
himself to us as the explanation, not of
Judaism only, but as the explanation of
all religion wherever found, as the full
revelation and incarnation of that after
which we have been feeling, the full
revelation of the power of an endless

life over men's fallen ambitions and fallen
hopes, the power that raises men from
the dead and brings life again to the sick
and weary. And the power is not after
a carnal commandment, not after the
laws of the past, but it is the power of
an endless life revealed in the person of
our Lord and Saviour Jesus Christ.

This power of an endless life has not
always been understood, and men have
often sought to explain it in such a way
that they have succeeded in explaining
it away. Men have tried to reduce Christianity to a very high code of morals.
Well, it is that. As soon as we are living upon the level of the sermon on the
mount the Kingdom of God will be very
nigh unto us. But it is not that only.
The Stoic philosophy gave us a code of
morals in many ways to be compared
with the code in the New Testament.
The code of Confucius does not fall very
far short in the formal directions of life

from those of Christ.   If Christianity
were only a code of morals, if it were
only the direction of what you and I
should do and should leave undone,
Christianity would not have had the
power over men's hearts and lives that
it has had; it would not have led to
right doing in the way it has done whenever faithfully proclaimed and accepted.
There must be some deeper and more
abiding explanation of the power of the
Christian religion over men's hearts and
lives than the explanation that would reduce it simply to a series of " Thou shalt
not," and " Thou shalt do this."   It is not
and never has been a mere code of morals.

Some have sought to find this power
in its wonderful reviving of philosophy.
But as a matter of fact Christianity did
not revive philosophy.   It only revived
certain phases of Greek philosophy, and
then often to Christianity's own great
disadvantage.   Again and again Chris-

tianity has been explained away with a
certain deliberateness of purpose by seeking to identify it in its essence with that
which any one may see to have been but
passing phases of a decadent Greek spirit.
Its power is not there. Its power has
been felt there. Its power has been felt
even in these decadent phases of Greek
thought, but it is not to be identified
with them in any sense; for Christianity
is more than a philosophy, it is more
than a system, it is more than a tradition,
it is more than an organization, it is more
than law, it is the power of an endless
life.

The great mistake of some of the early
centuries was to identify the Church
with an organization, to make its power
felt only through an organization; and
some, particularly one historian, who has
exercised great influence over the thinking of the English people, have sought
to show how by just coming at the right

time the religion of Jesus Christ was able
to subsidize the forms of an organization
already existing, and use it for its own
purposes.   If this explanation of the
power of Christianity is true, it is a very
strange circumstance that it was able
thus to appropriate to itself so powerful
an organization ; some explanation is due
us as to how the lesser thus swallowed
up the greater. But a little careful study,
I think, will show you that though this
organization was used by Christianity to
a large degree, Christianity used it to her
great and permanent disadvantage ; and
far from identifying Christianity with the
Roman power which it subsidized, far
from seeking its explanation in the power
of that empire which it overthrew, we are
to find in the very fact that it did too
closely identify itself with this falling
civilization the weakness which overtook
it and wellnigh led to its absorption in
the Middle Ages.

Christianity is more than the visible church. It is greater than the Roman Empire ; for the church had influence over men's hearts that the Roman Empire could not exercise. Christianity is centred in the divinity of its founder; it is centred in the fact that the Divine Life became incarnate. It has as its real secret the fact that there has arisen another priest, who hath been made, not after a carnal commandment, but after the power of an endless life. It is this incarnation as a common meeting ground between humanity and God that gives Christianity its uniqueness. This uniqueness does not consist in certain transcendental abstractions or metaphysical distinctions. The uniqueness of Christianity consists first in the inseparableness of Christ from humanity, and, second, in the inseparableness of Christ from Divinity; and on this common ground between God and man the divine

within us finds its expression in Jesus
Christ, the power of an endless life.

If you have followed the argument, I
wonder if you will be prepared to pass
with me to some of the more particular
applications of that truth to the life that
is about us. One of the difficulties of
all statement is that it may be made so
abstract that having made it and written
it down we close it up and put it away
upon our library shelves. But if it is
really true, if there is really a power of
an endless life, then it is for you and me
to come under its influence, — to feel it
ourselves, and make it a power felt in all
life.

Because there are so many substitutes
for this power of an endless life, it is
difficult for weak faith to grasp it and to
translate it into life. There is a substitute found in a certain intellectual destructiveness. We are soaked with the
critical spirit, we revel in pulling things

to pieces to see what is inside; and in
the process of our analysis we feel keenly
that triumphant sense that the little child
feels when she has torn her doll to pieces
and finds the saw-dust running out. We
find ourselves exulting over the things
we are analyzing. No man can take a
life,. or a character, or a history, or a
church, or a doctrine, or a creed, and
analyze it, without putting himself in a
certain position of judge as over against
it; and in that exalted position, even
though it is assumed by himself, he is apt
to find a certain satisfaction and pride,
which may lead him far astray. In our
present age there is this air of critical
analysis, of intellectual destructiveness,
of refined culture, and we are apt to
boast ourselves that we have found at
last some kind of substitute for this
power of which we hear so much down
the ages, and which the Nineteenth
Century would like exceedingly to do

without. Well, we can do without it
possibly for a little while, but not very
long. No age can do without it and do
its work. It is the one thing worth having, all else fades in significance in rela-
tion to it. The power of an endless life
alone brings all things into their proper
proportions. It shows the weakness of
mere critical analysis that, after we have
pulled our doll to pieces, we find ourselves sobbing over the ruins, face to face
still with the problems of death and dis-
solution, face to face still with shame and
unrighteousness and iniquity and oppression, our hearts still unsatisfied;
and we wonder if life is only this, — only
the satisfaction of pulling to pieces the
things that have pleased us for a moment,
and then leaving them, and going out
forever and forever without hope and
without God in the world. There is
nothing that we need so much as to get
away from our abstractions, our meta-

physics, our analysis and our culture,
and come face to face with the realities
of things ; and in our heart of hearts we
know, from the fact that it has had real
influence in our lives, that there is a
power of the Holy Ghost, that there is a
power of an endless life, that unless we
feel it and know it, unless it throbs in
our life, life is a failure.

There is another substitute which I
think is not less a real temptation. It is
found less in the cogitations than in the
active lives of men round about us. It
comes, I think, more vividly into the
foreground on the Fourth of July and
Washington's birthday, and other great
occasions for parading the wonderful
prosperity and material advancement of
the Nineteenth Century, and more particularly our portion of it. Let me call
it the commercial antichrist, — the sense
in men's hearts, that religion is a very
good thing in its way, but that there

are primary ends first to be reached;
that there is after all a real power in the
world, and that is the power of material
prosperity, which has to be attended to
first.   Then again, this heresy tells us
that men cannot conduct their business
unless they do this or that, and the principal thing is to conduct our business.
We have great confidence in ourselves
that once having attained our end, then
we can open the doors of heaven with
our gold and bribe the Almighty with
our successes; we will give him churches
and asylums and colleges, and leave him
large legacies in our wills.   There is
nothing that we need to come face to
face with more than this, — that the worship of the commercial antichrist is eat-
ing the hearts and lives out of men, and
that that worship must pass away, and
that only when it has passed away shall
we know in its fulness what is the power
of an endless life.   For all things pass

away. We are in the midst of the cosmic stream of prosperity only to find that our imperishable gold slips away. You treasure it up, and those who are most dear to you are corrupted and damned by it. You have worshipped it, and the image you have worshipped has fallen upon and crushed you. You have bowed to men for its sake, and they have turned upon you and accused you of the things they are doing themselves every day, because they dread the exposure which has come to you; and so shame and cursing have ever come because men know not the power of an endless life.

This is what we need to know; and if anything can teach it to us it would be a short review of the history we have been sketching. "All things pass away," says the writer to the Hebrews; nothing can be trusted, all things pass away. Only one thing remains, "Jesus Christ, the same yesterday, to-day, and forever."

Over against Jerusalem he stood, and
Jerusalem condemned him, and stretched
him on the cross, and said, " Ha! ha! we
have done once and for all with this de-
ceiver, we have nailed him upon a cross
of shame." Jerusalem passed into history, and Christ into history to make but
more manifest the power of an endless
life. The Romans took his followers and
made torches of them to light their gardens. The power of Rome passed away,
but the torches that lit their gardens sent
their light into the farthest North, re-
claiming men to righteousness, and even
barbarianism in all its brutality and ignorance felt the power of this endless life.
The Middle Ages said to themselves,
" We have found the last analysis!"
They too failed of their high aims; and
when brave monks spoke up they cast
them from their synagogues, and haughty
Rome sat a queen in her power and
laughed at the troublesome monks quar-

relling in their cells. But the power of
an endless life made itself manifest not
only in the Protestant North, it shook
even Catholic Rome, and called her
to face the bitter fact that if she would
not be destroyed she must hearken
to the voice of God. She hearkened,
and God spared her. He is speaking
yet, and Protestantism and Catholicism
have both to hear his voice in sorrowing
rebuke that they do not realize that the
power of all the past is this same power,
" Jesus Christ, the same yesterday, to-day,
and forever ; " a priest not after a carnal
commandment, not after the intellectual
destructiveness of the Nineteenth Century, not in accordance with our phi-
losophies, not in accordance with the
traditions of our ecclesiasticism, not in
accordance with our refinements in the
religious life, not in accordance with our
industrial wrongs, but after the real
power that is within every man that sub-

mits himself, crying aloud to his God to
make known the righteousness that is in
Christ Jesus, that our lives with all their
emptiness and poorness may be hidden
in the life that is in Jesus Christ. As
we look into his face sometimes it seems
to us there must be on that marred vis-
age a look of bitterness and despair that
we should have denied him thrice as we
have done; but he still pleads with us if
we only will hear his voice, saying to us,
" Come unto me, and find rest for your
souls," and know that through his cross,
his self-sacrifice, his self-denial, his righteousness is the full and free forgiveness
of our God, and that forgiving love is the
power of an endless life.

III.

CHRIST MADE PERFECT.

*Who, . . . though he was a Son, yet learned obe-
dience by the things which he suffered ; and having been made perfect, he became unto all them that
obey him the author of eternal salvation.* — HEB. v.
8, 9.

THE fulness of God's revelation is
such, and our capacity is so limited,
that every age and every generation, certainly every epoch, has new light from
heaven upon the path that man has made
dark. We ought ever to be learning
more of the way of God. We should be
ever seeking the revelation that God is
ever willing to grant in his Church, in
history, in our reasoning faculties, in the
study of his Scripture. There is, indeed,
the danger that, on the one hand, all that

is old may have such attraction for us
that we shall refuse to enter into the new,
and thus miss much of the revelation of
our God; and on the other hand, that we
may be so charmed with the novelties
that we shall forget the continuity of
God's revelation, and in seeking these
new things have only one-sided views of
truth.

We must therefore seek constantly the
truth in that which is old, and holding
fast the profession of our faith, press
forward into that which is new indeed
to our thinking, but old to the eternal
wisdom of our God. The process is the
same as spiritual process is everywhere.
Truth is borne in upon us; then we begin
to think about it, then we try to express
ourselves. When truth is borne in upon
us in the first instance, we are very likely
to be overwhelmed and confused; there
is more light than we can walk in. There
falls on us that same darkness and con-

fusion in the very midst of the glare of
the light that seems to have fallen upon
the disciples, and for a little while they
needed to draw aside that they might
rightly consider this new thought which
had been unfolded to them. The process,
then, of analysis finds our spirits often
in the critical mood. The moment we
begin to express the things that God has
been seeking to reveal to us, we find our
words quite inadequate for the purpose.
So it is rather the expression of the truth
that is progressive than the revelation
itself; rather that our capacity for seiz-
ing upon it develops gradually than that
God is giving us more and more light,
though that may also be said to be true.

The same thing is true in all art expression. You no doubt have had feelings that you would fain have expressed,
it may be of deep depression, of melancholy. You find your words inadequate;
but some one brings to your notice a

poem by some masterhand, and he not
only expresses the feeling in your heart
that was seeking a voice, but he reveals
to you a higher self, and deeper feelings,
of which you had only been either dimly
conscious or wholly unconscious until
the artist revealed them to you.

But even words have their limits.
And so it may be that a picture grasps
at your thought and expresses it as even
words cannot.   Take, for instance, such
a poem as that of Edgar Allan Poe's
"The Raven;" place it alongside the
marvellous print from the hand of Dürer
of "Melancholia," and see how the picture and poem answer one to the other,
expressing tones and feelings of your
thought that neither is able wholly to
articulate.   Even here there seems to be
a limit; but you chance to come where
music is being played.   Here words and
picture are supplemented with the tones
of the instruments.   Your spirit is caught

up, and the minor chord that sings through the refrain answers back to your spirit, and you rejoice that not only your emotions find expression, but that there has been revealed to you perchance the meaning and secret that is behind all emotion, so that your better and nobler self finds itself in the artistic expression of the moment.

So also on a higher plane is it true of God's revelation of himself in the person of Jesus Christ. There was very little danger that the disciples would forget the divinity of Jesus Christ; there was great danger that the world would do that. The danger was rather that the disciples would forget his humanity, and that danger Christ seems to have foreseen all through his ministry. It is his Sonship, it is his manhood, it is his limitations that he emphasizes in the midst of his devoted followers. How far he saw into history, church history tells you.

It was not his divinity, but his humanity that the Church forgot, and having
forgotten and laid it aside, the painted
image of the child, the Virgin Mary, or
the saints had to take the place that was
thus vacated, as revelations to man of
that link between him and the divinity
which he sought, but could truly find only
in the person of our Saviour Jesus Christ.
And so through many ages of church
history there was steadily lacking the
due emphasis upon this, the real humanity of our Saviour Jesus Christ. Christ
is the revelation not only of God to man,
but of man to his better self. Jesus
Christ is not only the fulness of the
Fatherhood revealed, he is also equally
emphatically a revelation of manhood as
it ought to be, the ideal of those things
for which in our better moments, when
the Spirit of God is moving upon our
spirits, we long to know and search after,
feeling that these things are eternal life.

Christ's humanity is emphasized all
through the New Testament. It is
not simply in his own words. We find
throughout the writings of Paul and of
John, throughout this letter to the Hebrews by an unknown author, throughout the whole literature of the New
Testament, a constant emphasis upon
the absolute humanity of our blessed
Lord and Saviour Jesus Christ. He
grew in wisdom; he knew not the times
and seasons; he did his miracles by the
authority of his Father; he thanked his
Father that he had been heard when he
cried to him before the tomb of Lazarus;
he knew his Father was able to save him
from death, and cried out in the bitterness of his agony, " If it be possible, let
this cup pass from me!" and he yielded
his will to the will of his Father, " Not as
I will, but as thou wilt." And so we
have Paul emphasizing the fact that he
took upon himself the form of a servant,

that he emptied himself and became man that he might enter into our hopes and fears; that he might enter into the very temptations, into your sorrows and my sorrows, and bleed with our bleeding hearts, and weep with our tears; that he might reveal unto us that better nature, that higher and diviner life, which has been clouded by our sinfulness, and can only be recovered by faith.

We find no stronger assertion of this absolute humanity than we do here in this letter to the Hebrews, and it is to this particular clause that I shall ask your more especial attention. "Who . . . though he was a son, yet learned obedience by the things which he suffered; and having been *made perfect*, he *became* unto all them that obey him the author of eternal salvation."

If any one were to ask you what the value of your life was, I have no doubt at all there would be many

responses of a different nature by those
who frankly answered. Some would say,
" Well, to be honest and frank, the whole
concern of my life just at present is my
business. These are times of depression, and there are many things I have to
neglect, and this is one thing I dare not
neglect. For my own sake, and for the
sake of my family, my business is at
present my chief concern." Ah! then,
my friend, you are not prospering in
business, no matter how much money
you may be making. If that is your
chief concern in life, then life, indeed,
has its solemn question to you, Is that
life worth living? Possibly you will say,
" Well, it is not so much my business as
my family. I live for my family; they
must be supported and cared for. This
is surely my chief duty; I should be worse
than infidel according to the sacred
writer if I did not care for those imme-
diately depending upon me." That is

very true ; but if this is your chief concern, you are not caring for them in the
best possible way : " He that loveth not
me more than father or mother, or sister
or brother, is not worthy of me." You
can care best for your family by not
making it the chief concern of your life.
You can care best for those whom you
love by not making them the real thing
for which you are living. Some of you
perhaps would be tempted to say, " It is
my country." I suppose, even in Chicago,
there would be some found loyal enough
to feel that the time of peace is more
dangerous for these United States than
the time of war. You say in your heart
of hearts, " It is my country which is my
chief concern." O patriot! you cannot
care for your country as you might if
it is the one thing for which you are living. There is a higher secret of life than
country or family or business, and that
higher secret can be learned only in the

study of the life and sufferings of our
Saviour Jesus Christ.

Let us turn to see what was the secret
of his life.   He learned in it !   That was
the thing !   You live that you may learn.
You are here, not to live for yourself, not
to die for yourself, but to learn,— to learn
the things that you cannot learn from business or in the home circle or from your
country.   You are here to learn to enter
into secrets and to find out mysteries, to
enter into the secret places of the Most
High ; you are here to make something of
your life ; you are here to be robed in a
robe of righteousness ; you are here to find
out secrets, not for yourself only, but for
others, — the high secrets of eternal wisdom ; you are here to learn, and unless
you are learning, though all these other
things may have their places in the
school of Christ, may be schoolmasters
to bring us to Christ, may have even
eternal value as they come into your

life, yet unless they are ministers of
righteousness, your life is so far forth a
failure.

Is life worth living? It depends upon
what description of life it is. The Christ
life was worth living; and just so far as
your life is the Christ life it is of value,
and just so far as it is not the Christ life
it is of no value whatsoever: " If the salt
have lost its savor, wherewith shall it be
salted ? "

What things did Christ learn? He
learned obedience, the basis of noble character. Let me venture a criticism upon
our American life and say that obedience
is one of the things lacking in our life,
that we are lawless as a people. We are
lawless in the home; we are lawless on
the street, and we need as a people to
learn obedience before we shall be fit
to command as we ought. Some of you
know what are the exercises on the fen-
cing floor or in the boxing-place. Possi-

bly some of you have seen the weariness with which the pupil constantly obeys the master's commands. Blow after blow, defence after defence, in barren, arbitrary sequence: " Oh! let me alone; I can do these things now by myself." But that is not the point. He must do the thing at once and in the exact moment of command. He must do it in obedience to the master's ruling, because the master knows that the pupil is soon to stand before one whose every movement is a command, whose every thrust must be met at once and sharply with the proper defence. He knows that the strife is one constant obedience to demands made upon him from the outside, and the pupil is not fit to control himself, is not fit to command his muscles, until he has learned by absolute obedience what will enable him in the conflict to answer with the proper defence every attack.

So at the basis of all worthy character

there is this absolute obedience; and it
is the only freedom. Lawlessness is not
freedom, license is not freedom; license
is slavery, lawlessness is worse than slavery. The only true freedom is obedience
to the highest, the search after the noblest,
the surrender of all to that which is infinite and eternal and unchangeable.

Christ came to teach us obedience.
And he taught it to us by learning obedience himself by the things which he
suffered. We are a little squeamish now
about some things. The doctors bear
some of the blame of that. The pain
that they relieve us of leads us to dread
any pain they cannot assuage, so that
the things we bore once with perfect
ease now seem to us large bugbears. I
do not know that on the whole this is
for evil; but, oh, friends, there is nothing
we need more than to be willing to bear
pain for others; than the power of sympathy to enter into the woes and pains of

5

those who are about us. There is nothing that you and I need more than to be
able to enter into the world's agony; and
in entering into it ours may seem a very
hopeless task; but even in the going with
others into the vale of darkness, the
touch of God through us may help them
to Christ. The kind word means more
than he who speaks it can know, to the
heart that is bowed down. There is an
immense amount of pain in this world
because from sheer, culpable ignorance
and sheer selfishness we cannot enter
into the woes of those about us. We
need to throw ourselves into the battle
of the world's tears and sorrows; we
need to know something of these bruised
hearts in their agony; we need to weep
with those who weep, that at last we may
rejoice with those who rejoice; we need
to learn obedience through the things
that we suffer ourselves, that we may be
able as Christ did to enter into the woes

of those who suffer. And so suffering
and pain have their sacred ministry; and
Christ came, not to be ministered unto,
but to minister. He took upon himself
the burden of the world's wild woe; he
entered into the trials and sorrows of
this life and was ground in the mad
machinery of man's devilish selfishness,
bigotry, and ignorance. In entire obedience to the mandates from above, he
learned obedience by the things which
he suffered, and has revealed to us a
higher manhood, a nobler ideal. He has
taught us that life is best worth living
when we too learn obedience through
the things which we suffer. He has
taught us that it is not in seeking our
own, nor in seeking to escape the world's
misery, nor in throwing off the burden of
its woes and pains, but in seeking the
extrication of the whole world from its
woe, that we shall find our highest life
and enter into the joy unspeakable of our
Lord.

So it was that Christ learned obedience through the things which he suffered, and has become the author of an
eternal salvation. Oh, surely there is no
nobler epitaph to be written over the
tomb of any one than that he served his
country and his God! There is no higher
ideal of manhood than that we enter into
the fulness of the salvation of which Jesus
Christ has become the author! It would
be glorious simply to enter into it; it
would be more glorious to take part in
the redemption. Who are we to be
counted worthy of this? And yet Christ
has called us to it, and we are to fill
up in our bodies that which is lacking of
the sufferings of Christ for his body's
sake, which is the Church. We with
Christ are to become the redemption of
the world. Suffering as he has taught us
to suffer; dying as he has taught us to
die; living as he lived; walking with him;
knowing what true manhood is because

he has revealed it unto us; learning
obedience by the things which we suffer,
we shall enter with him as his brethren,
called no more his servants but his
brethren; taking part with those whom
his blood has washed from their stains.

This, dear friends, is the meaning of
life. This is the bringing in of the eternal salvation. This is the one secret
of the establishment of God's kingdom.
I know not the hearts of those before
me: who can enter into the secret places
of another's life? But I know enough of
life to know that there is no one heart
before me, even the youngest, which has
not had its woe. I know there is no one
before me to whom life has not from time
to time become a weary entanglement and
a maze that seems hopelessly ensnarled.
Dear friends, if life were perfectly plain
we should never learn; we should never
know. It is because of this entanglement that we feel the awful burden of

our helplessness, and groan within ourselves waiting for the redemption. To
you that redemption is proclaimed.
" Freely ye have received, freely give."
God has forgiven you: walk in the forgiven life; know him; choose him; learn
from these very sufferings, from these
very mistakes and tangled mysteries, the
obedience that is freedom, the life that is
eternal salvation. May God help us, and
grant us his grace and his peace.

IV.

THE IMPULSIVE TYPE OF CHRISTIANITY.

Simon, Simon, behold, Satan asked to have you, that he might sift you as wheat: but I made supplication for thee, that thy faith fail not: and do thou, when once thou hast turned again, stablish thy brethren. — LUKE xxii. 31, 32.

FROM the very fact that Christianity is a life, we see that it expresses itself in a variety of ways. From the very first Christianity has been the synthesis, the gathering and putting together, of a great many tendencies and forces animated by one impulse. From the very first, different elements have entered into it; some to aid, some to hamper its development. The infinite wisdom of God provided so that every variety of character, and the impulses of affection, of law, of intellect,

might all be used for the building up
and strengthening of his kingdom on
earth.   We shall expect, therefore, to find
throughout Christian history, both in
its beginning and in its progress, very
great differences in types of character.
No one man gathers into himself all the
fulness of the revealed truth.   We shall
find as we study the biography of the
New Testament that in a wonderful way
the various types of character are baptized and redeemed, and, at the same
time, they preserve marvellously their individual peculiar characteristics, bringing
these with them into the service to which
God has called them.

We do not know so much about the
work that Peter did in the early Church
as we do concerning the work of Paul,
because the second part of the Acts and
the Epistles of Paul are the material upon
which we rely mainly for our account of
the early Church, and these of course

dwell largely upon the subject of Paul's labors and activities. But, at the same time, there is enough left us to show that Peter was a very strong, a very dominant element in that part of the Church which centred around Jerusalem, and which influenced Bithynia and the more eastern parts of Asia Minor.

The traditions about Peter's life are not very trustworthy. We do not find very many traditions at all concerning him until about one hundred years after his death ; and then, although the traditions are many, they can be nearly all traced back to one source, so that we have not the advantage of a great many witnesses. These traditions are moreover often so evidently foolish and untrustworthy that it is very difficult to build up any scheme of his Christian activity upon the basis of them.

But we do not need to go to any traditional story of Peter's life to get a definite impression of the man. His is one of the marked characters of the New Testament's wonderful series of portraits, taking them merely as literature. It is marvellous with what distinctness character is etched throughout the Old and New Testaments! How many masterpieces we have of character sketches, a few words giving a whole character! This is true, for instance, of the patriarchs. It is true also throughout the Old Testament history, sometimes the whole life and activities of a king being gathered together in two or three verses in a perfectly marvellous way.

With a few touches we have Peter's character painted before us with a distinctness that it is hard to find the equal of anywhere in literature. Peter is a man essentially of impulses. Energetic, marvellously useful along these lines, but, like a good many impulsive people, not very trustworthy, not to be always counted upon. Peter is the first to come to Jesus walking upon the water, but very soon sinks because his faith gives way. Peter is the very first to draw his sword in defence of the Master, — is the only one to spring to his defence, but denies him to the maid at the door. Peter is the first to speak, but not always the wisest when he speaks. Peter is very ready to answer the question as to who Jesus is, — " Thou art the Messias," but he is also very apt to take Christ aside and rebuke him, when the Messias tells about the suffering which lies before him. Peter in his impulsiveness will not have Christ wash his feet, and in equal impulsiveness would have him wash his hands and his head that he might be all consecrated to the Master's service.

This is characteristic of Peter not simply before Christ's death; but even after his death, in his epistles, we find the same characteristics. Peter is one of the very first to try to bridge the gulf between the Gentile and Jewish Christian churches, but one of the very first to retreat ignominiously from the position he had taken, when he is in Antioch surrounded by those who say to him, " Thou being a Jew, eatest with those who have not been circumcised." And Paul withstood him to the face because he was, in his very impulsiveness, in his very superficiality, in danger of permitting that to be done which would have left the Christian Church in chains, and would have hampered irretrievably its progress.

We find that Peter is impulsive; and yet we need impulsiveness, and we have to take it with its weakness and with its strength. There is an impulsive Christianity which is one of the largest and most needed factors in the building up of the healthy Christian life. Impulsive Christianity has indeed weakness, with

which we have to reckon. The man of
impulses is a little like the kindling with
which you kindle your fire. You might
use a whole box of matches in trying to
set fire to the coals, and you could not do
it. Take a little kindling, strike your
match, and you soon have a steady glow.
It is true you could not very easily warm
your house with kindling, but at the same
time you could not very easily warm your
house without it. Impulsive Christianity is very needful to set fire to the forces
that are in God's providence regenerating
the world. Impulsive Christianity will
have indeed its weakness in that like
Peter it is very much in danger of denying the Master. The man of impulses is
very apt to find himself stranded by
waves of a strength he has not taken
accurate reckoning of; but, at the same
time, every great religious movement has
commenced with the fiery, impulsive elements of the community. It was the

impulsive Cornish miners who gave the
key-note to the evangelical revival whose
blessed force is not ended yet. It was
the impulsive classes in North Germany
that caught fire first when a lonely monk
defied the Romish power and proclaimed
liberty to the captive. It was the impulsive classes in this country who heard the
preaching of Finney, who accepted him
with all his extravagance, with all his
weaknesses, with all his want of accurate
thought. They accepted him because
they felt his was a message from on high,
that touched men's hearts with something better than the old dogmatism on
which the Church was starving herself to
death, a message that set this country on
fire ; and after it was set on fire, there
were steadier forces to complete and
carry on the movement to a better and
higher issue, out of which has come so
much that has meaning for our national
and individual life.

We shall have to take the impulsive man and impulsive Christianity into account because they form a large element even of the most reflective life. We would not give anything for a man who did not have impulses, even though they were not always wise. We would not care to have even a wise man as our dearest friend, if a cold, calculating intellect was all you had to deal with. Impulses, even if sometimes they are wrong, if sometimes they do disturb our judgment, so that our emotions get the better of our calculations, are divine factors in character building. Our calculations are not infallible any more than our impulses, and sometimes it is a good thing to give our emotions free scope, and learn from mistakes to guide them better, but not to suppress them.

We have to take into account impulses because they are a force for good or for evil. There is an impulsive class that

will make itself felt, and it will make itself
felt for the kingdom of evil unless it is
baptized and captured for Christ.   There
were some men of impulse no doubt in
the throng that cried: "Allelujah! Ho-
sanna to the Son of David!" and then,
" Crucify him ! crucify him !" but Peter,
even if he did deny his Lord, did not cry,
" Crucify him !"   One man of impulse
at least had been captured for Christ,
for the future kingdom, for the glory of
the cross ! We need to see to it that
our Christianity is not purely reflective,
is not purely intellectual ; is not pure cal-
culation, is not pure thought. We need
impulses ; we need holy impulses. We
need to feel their throbs in our life ; we
need, indeed, sometimes to know the bene-
fits of impulsive repentance.   It is good
for us sometimes to go out with Peter into
the lonely quiet at cock-crowing and yield
to the impulsive bitterness of our emotions, pouring out our soul in the agony

of repentance because our lives have so
often been a betrayal of the consecrated
trust God has committed to every one
of us to keep against that day. And I
should not wonder, if we knew Peter's
influence better we should find out that
he was a strength to all the brethren
because of his very sympathy with them.
I think that underlies Christ's remarks to
Peter. He says: "Lovest thou me more
than these!" He did not simply rebuke
him. Peter had been professing his loy-
alty so very pronouncedly, possibly those
who sometimes were his rivals, his former
partners in his fishing concerns, may
have felt he was a little too forward.
"Now," says Christ, "when thou art converted, strengthen thy brethren." It is
for the most part the man of emotions,
the man whose heart is largest, that is
felt in the time of trouble to come closest
to us and to strengthen us most in our
hour of need. What warm sympathy

Peter must have had with those who
touched him, who, like himself, were apt
to betray the Master in the stress of
their temptation! Peter, I have no
doubt, was many a time able to take
some weaker Christian than himself
and help him up, saying to him, " You
know very well the story of my betrayal,
but Christ has not given me up.   No,
he said to me, ' Feed my lambs; feed my
little sheep.'   He looked me straight in
the eye, he took me by the hand, he
helped me up, and he will help you up."
Peter, I have no doubt, was able to
strengthen the brethren as some of those
who had sinned less were not able to
strengthen them, because of his sympathy, because he was able to enter into
their lives and weaknesses and to take
account of the yielding of our whole
nature under the stress of temptation.
When so tempted we are able almost to
cry out with Paul, " It was not I that did

it, but the flesh: therefore, the thing I would, that I do not; and the thing I would not, that I do."

We need emotional Christianity, with all its errors of judgment, that we may come closer to one another and feel with one another. With kindled emotions and kindly impulses we need to go to one another and help one another up, even though the cooler, calculating judgment will often speak about the hopelessness and helplessness of it.

Christ on his cross felt also what it was to surrender his spirit, and the dear loved ones round about him with all their weakness, into the keeping of his Father. God needs us, even in our weakness. He needs all that there is of us. He needs the weakness; if it is committed to him, if it is crucified with Christ, if it is baptized unto his death, God can use it, and will use it in good time.

And when we are converted, let us

strengthen our brethren. We need that
sympathetic, impulsive Christianity, because it comes first, and will often go further than the more calculating kind. John
got first to the sepulchre, but it was Peter
that entered in. John first recognized
Christ, but it was Peter who jumped into
the water to go to him. Impulsive, emotional Christianity is needed because it
has power to carry us on, sometimes even
to victory that seems wellnigh hopeless.
God can cleanse and baptize our emotions, and send them further and faster
than our poor weak judgments may deem
safe in the beginning. We need to baptize our best and noblest impulses; we
need to baptize our emotions; we need to
commit them to God, to have them lifted
up, sanctified and made a burning fire.

This age prides itself upon being reflective, analytical, critical. So it is.
That has all its place. Sometimes we are
a little fond of staying back rather than

setting ourselves against the wrong:
"Dear me! we ought to do so and so.
We ought to do this and that. Somebody ought to go in and purify our politics!" A crying need of the world to-
day is a baptized indignation at wrong-
doing. We need to feel that God can
use us when we are set on fire for him.
He will take care of the judgment, quick-
ening and sharpening it in the fires of
enthusiasm, by which we will set fire to
the world. Our impulses for righteousness need obedience.

We need to have our emotions touched.
There is something very wonderful to me
in the way in which the cross of Christ
seems to have affected the northern barbarism. One might hardly think that
those wild, ferocious, blood-stained Northmen, accustomed to every sort of cruelty,
to every sort of iniquity, could be reached
on the side of their emotions. Yet it
was not those skilled in ecclesiastical

orthodoxy that reached the North. It
was not an elaborately reasoned system
that touched these men. What really
touched the north of Europe was a band
of brave but ill-trained monks, who went
holding up simply the cross on which was
nailed the suffering, bleeding body of
Christ. They were touched by that story
of atoning love as you would hardly have
thought these great brawny, blood-stained
Northmen could have been touched; and
once touched, they became the ethical
power that broke the chains from off the
Church and set Europe free. We need
to have Christ lifted up, not only that our
intellects may be true, but that our hearts
may be touched with the message of
God's everlasting and infinite love, show-
ing itself forth in the suffering and patience of our Lord and Saviour Jesus
Christ. We need again and again to
be converted by looking at the cross and
seeing there all the love of the incarnate

God, that we may be ready to crucify with him our impulses, our passions, our affections, our lives; that we may look into his face and be able to answer truly, " Lord, thou knowest all things. I have been wicked and sinful and untrue to thee. My heart is wellnigh hardened with selfishness and self-deceit; but I would have thee touch me, I would have thee draw me closer to thyself. Thou knowest all things; thou knowest that I love thee." May God help us to con-secrate our emotions to the service of Christ. May God help us to hear the word that has come to many a weak and wavering Peter: " Simon, Simon, Satan hath desired to have thee, that he may sift thee as wheat: but I have prayed for thee, and when thou art converted, strengthen thy brethren."

V.

THE INTELLECTUAL TYPE OF CHRIS-
TIANITY.

With freedom did Christ set us free : stand fast
therefore, and be not entangled again in a yoke
of bondage. — GAL. v. i.

PAUL swept into himself in a very
remarkable way the three world
influences, — the Greek, the Roman, and
the Jewish. One of the great historians
of Germany has pointed out that in
these three world influences we have the
practical explanation of all that we value
as civilization. He was a Roman citi-
zen. There are, I think, decided traces
throughout both Romans and Galatians
that he was fairly well acquainted with at
least the principles of Roman law. His
knowledge of Greek poetry we are possibly inclined to exaggerate because of such

chance quotations from it as we find
in his writings; but, at the same time, it
is not at all unlikely that he was familiar with the literature of Greece, for in
his own native city of Tarsus Greek
influences were the predominant ones.
Tarsus was a city that had had a great
deal of influence, and its influence was
very largely intellectual. It had been
greatly attracted by Greek thought; so,
for instance, the games of Tarsus were
in all likelihood prevalently Greek rather
than Roman, which would indicate a
predominance of Greek rather than
Roman thought.

Of course, Paul was Jewish, and thoroughly Jewish; a Pharisee brought up
in the Pharisaic schools, thoroughly acquainted with the history of his people,
thoroughly imbued with the best spirit
of his own time. Thus we have a very
remarkable figure, combining in one centre the synthesis of the great influences

that were to mould the destiny of the nations of the earth.   It was natural, therefore, that Paul should make for himself
an intellectual atmosphere in which the
Church's thinking was to develop.   He
did for the Church what neither James,
nor John, nor Peter could have done so
far as we know them.   It was quite impossible for even the wonderful Fourth
Gospel and the writings of John to
have quite the effect upon the Roman
mind that Paul's writings were able to
exercise, in part through the limitations
of the Roman mind, and also, indeed,
owing to the limitations of the intuitive
and perceptive character of John's mind.

We take Paul, therefore, very naturally as the type of what we may call intellectual Christianity.   Christianity must
be intellectual if it is to command the
respect of men whom God would save.
Christ will have the whole of man ; he
will have his mind, and his heart, and

his life. Christ's kingdom is not a one-sided kingdom. It is to be social, it is to be intellectual, it is to be moral, it is to be spiritual, it is to be rounded out. The intellect must be fired from above; and once fired from above, it enters forthwith into the Christian life as a very large and very important factor.

But the intellectual type of Christianity has of course its dangers. The intellectual life has a certain tendency to arrogance that is born and bred of the constant comparison of its own self with the grosser stupidity which it finds round about it. A man does not need to be very far on in the intellectual life before he begins to compare himself with others, greatly to his own advantage, however, and to the disadvantage of those whom he has left behind. The danger of intellectual arrogance is especially perceptible in the mind that is clear and logical. The mind that having started

with certain terms must carry its reasoning on to the end has no patience with
the mind that insists on breaking in with
other lines of thought before the solution
is given.

Intellectual Christianity has also its
dangers in the fact that the intellectual
life is very apt to exclude us from some
other phases of life. The man who is a
mere intellectual machine cannot enter
into many of the hopes and fears and
wishes of the multitude about him, for the
multitude is not governed in the first
instance by the intellect. If we were
quite shrewd enough we should realize
that the intellect must come after a great
deal else, for the intellect is analytical, and
if there is not something to analyze it has
no place at all. But this is too often forgotten, and the danger to thinking men is
a certain dogmatic narrowness, a certain
hardness, and conventional type even, so
that we find that intellectual Christianity

as it has come down the ages has often
repelled instead of attracting even those
to whom intellectual Christianity ought to
have had power and value.

I think you will notice in Romans and
Galatians a tone somewhat different from
that which you will find in Philippians
and Ephesians, and different also from the
personal tone of the pastoral letters. No
thoughtful mind can fail to see that there
was progress, decided progress, in the
spiritual life of Paul. When we leave
the first and second centuries and turn
to such men as Tertullian and Augus-
tine, and in the seventeenth century to
such men as the scholastics and the intellectual leaders of the Reformation, we
are thoroughly and powerfully impressed
with a certain intellectual narrowness of
dogmatism, and a harsh and arrogant
tone, which shows us that on the intellectual side of Christianity there are dangers
which it is scarcely possible to avoid, no

matter on which side of the controversy
we stand, unless we are fully baptized
with the spirit of the Lord Jesus Christ,
and have made intellectual surrender to
him as well as surrender of the heart.

Intellectual Christianity from the very
nature of the thing is analytical, and analysis is the pulling apart. From the very
nature of it intellectual Christianity has
in it a certain destructive element. It
must criticise, it must look behind, it is
never satisfied with the forms as they are
round about. It could not be, it would
cease to be, intellectual Christianity if it
did not thus insist, and sternly insist,
upon satisfying the conditions of God-
given reason. But there is the danger
that it may confine itself to the destructive, and that the constructive work be
left out of account, — to the pulling to
pieces of Sadduceeism with nothing as
yet to put in its place. But for all that,
we must take it as it is. We enter the

Christian life with our reason, and we must take our reason along with us. The forms of reason we cannot leave behind any more than we can leave other forms behind. When you first took Christ into your life, you took him with your many defects, which Christ in your heart is going to cure daily if you will surrender yourself daily unto him. There are faces about us that you have perhaps seen grow beautiful because of the life of suffering and sacrifice that has changed the plain features into a heavenly beauty. But we cannot start with our faces shining. We cannot start with anything but reason as God has given it to us. Paul had to start in his Christian course as a Pharisee. He had to leave much behind; but it was because he surrendered his reason, surrendered it wholly to Christ, that it was changed and transformed into one of the mightiest and most potent weapons for the winning of the victory

of the Church and for the building up of
the temple whose strengthening God had
entrusted to his servant.

And so I think we can not go far
astray in taking Paul as a splendid type
of the proper use of the intellect, and as
the proper intellectual type of Christianity. This is evident, because Paul
brought to the service of Christ everything he had, — his learning, his Pharisaic training, his knowledge of Greek
thought, his knowledge of the Hebrew
language; and he laid it all as a sacrifice on the altar to his Master. His
intellect, his intellectual powers, these
were his Master's, because everything
he had was his; and what splendid
use he made of them! Take, for instance, that scene upon Mars Hill.
This little Jewish man, probably rather
unsightly, if tradition is correct, who
comes to Athens, where every one is
so graphically described as seeking only

to hear some new thing. He met these Athenians with their scientific dogmatism, with their philosophical problems; they amused themselves with these things and believed that they were living, precisely as a great many of us to-day amuse ourselves by haunting the lecture-rooms and discussing questions, without any real intention of making them bear upon our lives or, through us, upon other people's lives. They were at Athens, as we should find them in New York and Boston and Chicago to-day, and to this intellectual centre the despised Jew comes. They will hear what this babbler says. And could anything have been more calculated to win their attention than the tact with which he commences to speak of the things they believe in common, leading them up to the things he had come to proclaim as the one message worth telling? It is a study for every Christian apologist, for every Chris-

tian missionary, for every Christian minister. I suppose that some of those who
have objected to the Parliament of Religions would have found great fault with
Paul for quoting heathen philosophers,
and setting the seal of his approval to
what they said. How could any one ever
have complimented these empty-hearted,
though overburdened Athenians upon
their being too religious! But Paul is
all things to all men, and he catches
them; he gets their attention at least long
enough to tell them that the things he
had come to proclaim were what they
were hungering for, the things of the
risen life, and he tells them of the resurrection from the dead. He is a splendid
type of what intellectual Christianity
ought to be, because, bringing as he did
all things to Christ, and laying all things
upon that altar, his intellectual life is a
means to an end, and that only. There
is a tendency in us to grade all things.

We say, "How much higher is the artistic than the purely intellectual; how much higher the intellectual than the practical! How nice it is to see men who have been absorbed in business give now their time to intellectual work!" As though intellectual work were any better than business! There would be no intellectual work if there were no business. And so we set ourselves up in little exclusive ranks, — the agricultural, the poor farmer, he is one class by himself, — and lose sympathy entirely in our arbitrary, exclusive distinctions, which ought to be lost in the feeling that humanity is one, that there is no man mean in the sight of God. Intellectual work may be as exclusive, as selfish, as ignoble, as material, as debased, as any other work in the world if it is not brought to the altar of Christ; if it is not sanctified by the presence of God's Holy Spirit; if it is not unselfish, and wholly unselfish, as a means to some greater end for the great throbbing life of which we are a part, and from which to cut ourselves off is spiritual suicide. God is in life, and if we would come in contact with God we must be in contact with that life which is his, and is all around us.

So then, whatever may be our intellectual attainments, we have only to compare ourselves with Omnipotence to realize how pitiable and painfully stupid the wisest among men have been in all the ages. How puerile seems the reason we have counted fine! how mistaken the dogmas men have said would last forever! how utterly wrong the generalizations men have thought they had established! Let us prostrate ourselves before God, and find that the intellect is of use only as God takes it and enlightens it and makes it the means, as he made Paul's splendid intellect the means, for making known the message of salvation through a risen Lord to a world lying in wickedness.

And this also is to be learned from Paul, that throughout his life he not only seemed to use his intellectual life as a means to an end, but he never misused it. It is never thrust upon us, it is kept ever as a means to an end, and he is constantly and forever surrendering it to the one thing, — to the voice within him that speaks to men, and tells them that right is right and wrong is wrong to all eternity.

So Paul used his intellect, and I believe that in the using of it for the purposes of Christ it received not only baptism but training; that even for the purposes of the intellect, to surrender it to God is the best thing we can do. I believe this is true along the whole range of life. It was when art began to be practised merely for art's sake that it not only became decadent, but the na-

tional life became decadent. Mr. Ruskin
points out, but to me seems to offer no
adequate explanation of the fact, that at
the time art has reached its highest expression, the national life has seemed
generally to be most decadent, as in the
Augustan era, the Renaissance in Italy,
the period of Queen Anne in England.
This, however, seems to me to be one of
the solutions of it, that the age was decadent because art was practised simply for
art's sake, and intellectualism was practised merely for the intellect's sake. As
soon as a man attends to his body merely
for his own sensuous bodily purposes,
just so soon not only is there decadence
of the best that is in him, but there will
be decadence of the body, decadence of
the mind, decadence of all that is essential to real life; and if art must express
life, that life must be divine to be worth
expressing, and until we learn to treasure what is divine, we shall find our-

selves again and again upon the weary slope up which men have crawled with so much difficulty only to find the burden dragging them down when they believed they saw eternity from the top.

God needs our intellects, and never more so than to-day. We need to surrender our intellects to God that the pressing problems of the Church may be solved. We stand divided. We have been hair-splitting and fighting among ourselves, and the great world outside neither fears nor hates us. There is no task more precious in the sight of God to-day than the task the men of intellect have before them in the solving of problems whose solution will unite us once more in the face of the enemy, and thrust us, even if we be cut in pieces, in the face of the foe with the banner of Christ and his Cross over us. Young men, some of you with educational advantages of which to your dying day you will have to render an account unto the Father, take these advantages, take your minds, and make them a sacrifice upon the altar of the Lord Jesus Christ. There is no more splendid use of the consecrated, surrendered intellect than the solving of the weary social problems that lie before us. Christ saw how it would be with us. He said, "The poor ye have always with you, but me ye have not always." It is just because Christ is not always with us that the poor are always with us. We have problems that need more than mere goodness, that need more than impulsive Christianity, that need more than simply the heart that goes out in pity and sympathy; we need surrendered intellects; we need consecrated brains; we need directing minds baptized from on high; we need you business men to take and reform our accursed social and industrial conditions. Must man be ever groaning

in the weary tread-mill of life, finding
those who are on the top corrupted by
the eminence, and those below ground
to death by the weight? The world
needs your intellects set on fire from on
high, and never more than to-day. We
need to surrender them to God. What
the world needs is not surrender to a
church, nor to a priest, nor to a theological school, nor to a general assembly, but
to God only. "Stand fast in the liberty
wherewith Christ hath made us free, and
be not entangled again in the yoke of
bondage." That surrender must be absolute. Who are we that we should
strive with the Almighty? Who are we
to think that we are sufficient in ourselves? Our only use, our only dignity,
our only worth, will come from our lives
being the expression of the divine life
which breathes into our human minds the
message of God's love for his fallen crea-
tion. For God can redeem it, if it will

only suffer itself to be redeemed. God over all — even though he is crucified — preached to all nations. God over all, and Christ at the right hand of the Father, who will come again to receive a redeemed universe gathered into his Church that we may be his sons and daughters.

Dear friends! Young men! Young women! what are you doing with your minds? What are you doing with your culture? What are you doing with the life God has given you? What are you doing with your advantages? These things are responsibilities which will weigh you down before the judgment-seat unless you share them with Christ, unless you are working his law in the world. May God help you to do it!

VI.

THE ETHICAL TYPE OF CHRISTIANITY.

*Take, brethren, for an example of suffering and of
patience, the prophets who spake in the name of
the Lord.* — JAS. v. 10.

I HAVE taken this text because the type
of Christian life represented by James is
as it were, the connecting link between
the Old Testament and the New. The
logic of the life of Christ, of his teachings
and sufferings, was a glorious manifestation of that liberty which is in Christ
Jesus, and of which we see Paul to be so
splendid a type. But Christ himself left
those who were to come after him, under
the guidance of the Spirit promised, to
find their way to the logic of that position. He himself attended the synagogue; he proclaimed himself as the

fulfilment and not the destruction of
the Old Testament; and it is very easy
for us to leave the light of the New Testament and greatly exaggerate the gap
that separates the Old and New Testaments from each other. We might very
easily altogether misunderstand the New
Testament or misinterpret the Old by
taking either of them separately, not re-
membering that in the revelation of
himself God has used the Old Testament as a preparation, and that the full
importance of this revelation is only
to be realized when we view it as developed in Jesus Christ in the New
Testament.

There was a section of the Christian
Church that was not in accord with the
complete logic of the Christian position
as set forth by Paul. It was very natural that the Jewish Christian church
should resent many things, find fault
with many things, and fail to understand

many things that came quite naturally to
the Christian Church that had broken
loose more completely from the old life
that still centred in Jerusalem. There
was antagonism; which antagonism was
bridged over by the wisdom and patience
of the principal apostles; but the antagonism made itself felt, of which we have
evident signs in the New Testament
history itself.

It is James that represents a type of
thought that is the intermediate link between the old dispensation and the new,
as represented by the Jewish Christian
wing of the Church. It was only after
the destruction of Jerusalem that the
Church, as it were, broke into the fulness of the life, the fulness of the liberty, the glory of the revealed form of
Christ's gospel. James, however, represents a type of Christian life that, with
all its limitations, with all its necessary
defects, has had a very glorious history

in God's Church, a history that is not
yet completed. The type represented by
James will, I believe, always have its
message and its mission to the Christian
world. James represents what we might
know as the Puritan type of the Christian
life, — a type of Christian character whose
praises have been sung and whose limitations have been pointed out so frequently,
that it has become to us usually either
a bugbear on the one hand, or an idol
on the other. The truth is between the
two. The Puritan type of Christian character had its invaluable message to the
Christian world; it had a heroic work;
and with all its limitations, its work may
have to be done over and over again by its
resurrection in the Church of God, speaking, warning, and living the life which
has proved in the crises of the Church's
history of such momentous importance.

The limitations of the Puritan type of
Christian life lie somewhat on the sur-

face.   There is an attachment to the formal elements that has its cause in the history of the rise of the Puritan type.   It
rose as a protest.   The Jewish Christian
church was also a protest.   This church
did not seek to separate itself from the
synagogue, nor from the sacrifices and
the temple.   To the very end it worshipped at the temple.   Paul goes up at
the demand of the Jewish Christian
church to fulfil his vows, taking part in
the temple services.   They were the reform party in the Jewish church,—a party
that did not care to break loose from the
old, but sought to rehabilitate it, sought
to breathe into it a newer spirit, protesting against its weakness and rottenness;
and in that protest there are the elements of some of the limitations which
have marked them.   They became the
protesting or Protestant church, missing
some of the tenderness, and much of the
formative spirit, and in the very vigor of

their assaults becoming critical and destructive, rather than formative, in their character.

This weakness may be seen, I think, in what the Puritan type has done for England, where it has appeared more frequently and in greater purity than in any other Christian civilization. The Puritan type there has attached itself to certain individual and distinct reforms. It has begun in protesting against particular lines of thought; it has had its force and strength from its pointed, direct, and uncompromising attack upon particular and visible evils. In doing this, whether it gained its point or lost it, it has been in danger from this undue emphasis upon its purely protesting character, and in the second and third and fourth generations of Puritanism the danger has been that each generation lived more and more upon the protest and the traditions of the past, and so failed to comprehend the new duty which was to take the place of the things which had been destroyed. Hence it has been that Puritanism too often in the life of the second or third generation has been marked by a vacuum which has not always been filled with those things which were most useful to the Christian Church as a whole.

Then, also, this ever protesting characacter of the Puritan type has always brought with it the danger of a certain sternness in its righteousness, that sometimes has produced a sense of self-righteousness and censoriousness extremely detrimental to the entirety of character. In the protesting, there has been a constant tendency to self-assertion, first, indeed as against the world and evil, a self-assertion that is justified by facts; but then, as a consequence of that, a self-assertion as against any one that differs with it,— a self-assertion too apt to regard anything that opposes it as necessarily

an evil. Hence, there has always been
in the literature of Puritanism in its later
manifestations a certain narrowness that
has been one of the marked weaknesses
often pointed out. There has also been
a certain lack of tenderness, a certain
lack of the fine flavor that characterizes
Paul, for instance, and still more John in
his writings; a tenderness one feels to
be indeed out of place upon some battle-
fields; a tenderness that it is only natural
that men should lay aside when they enter
into the sterner contests that Puritanism
has so often waged. At the same time a
lack of this tenderness has left Puritanism often out of touch with the newer
life, has isolated it, has made it often the
embodiment of a religious type that with-
draws itself from the world in a way in
which Christ did not withdraw himself
from the world. This has exposed it to
the charges of bigotry and straight-laced-
ness, and even of hypocrisy, because in

its isolation being out of touch with the
world, not in sympathy with the move-
ments round about it, it has often yielded
unconsciously to other evils than those
against which it was called into being to
protest against. And so it has exposed
itself to the ready charge of deep incon-
sistency; and, as we see in the repre-
sentative Puritanism of England, two or
three times these charges have been so
successfully emphasized that Puritanism
seemed for the time to have lost all its
moral and religious value.

After we have pointed out these limitations, it will be proper also to remind
you that the type of Christianity which
we have called Puritanism, and which I
think is here represented in James, has
its mission and its message. This very
righteousness is the glory of such a letter
as this, and the Puritan theocracy at the
time of Cromwell has as its glory and its
strength, that it emphasized certain cle-

ments in our Christian life that have too
often failed of emphasis when the Church
has been either prosperous, or swinging
along in an easy rut. Often have men
failed to see, what the Puritan type
sees clearly, the danger and the ruts '
that lie so much in front of us all along
the way. James has a message, first, to
those who are tempted and tried; and
there is in his message a little of that
stern impatience with the weakness of
the unstable man. There is something
of the rigor and vigor of the Puritan
spirit which feels that manhood means
courage and strength, and that Christian
manhood is to be undaunted courage and
undaunted strength. What do you lack?
Why do you whine? Why do you complain? Let a man rather count himself
as in the way of grace when he is in the
way of trials and temptations. If he lack
wisdom, let him ask of God, who giveth
freely to every man; but be brave, cour-

ageous and undaunted; know this, that
our God is a consuming fire, and in his
strength we may have hope and grace for
ever and for evermore. There is some
fibre, there is some muscle, there is some
strength, there is some vigor, in the very
type of doctrine that is represented by
James, and which has been emphasized
with such care by the Puritan type
throughout Christian history. There is
need of that message. Constantly ought
we to emphasize this need for vigor; for
an undaunted and unflinching courage
of our convictions, a courage to do right,
a righteousness that trusts forever, that
does not waver, a conception of Jehovah
as King of kings and Lord of lords,
with whom to fight, for whom to struggle
is blessedness and courage itself. Let
not that man who doubteth think he
shall receive anything: he is like the
surge of the sea, driven by the wind and
tossed. It was not characteristic of the

Puritan to be tossed around like the
wave of the sea. Over and over again
he has unsheathed his sword and stood
for that which he considered right and
against wrong and iniquity even in high
places. There is a message of Puritanism that rings down English history
which has given strength to the democracy, which has not feared king or
priest, which has not feared traditions,
which has feared nothing but Jehovah ; a
note that we need here from time to time
amidst our notes of triumphs and rejoi-
cings. Our victory over sin is not completed; we have still to see struggles;
righteousness is not yet crowned; the
cross is yet to be borne. Protestantism
has its struggles yet before it. I verily
believe that in this country the time will
come when there will be need again for
the Puritan spirit. It will be a blessing
to this country when men stand up for
righteousness, seeking one another, and

standing united for the justice of God, and when they feel that this letter of James is an epistle of inspiration upon which they can base their claims for a higher life, a higher purity, a higher freedom from the subtle corruptions and temptations which so often sap the Christian manhood, which so often weaken the Christian character.

And again, Puritanism has some special messages. I think it is rather characteristic of the Puritan spirit that it does pick out and specially emphasize special evils. James has a message to the different classes, — to the wealthy in danger of abusing their wealth, to the intelligent in danger of relying upon their intellects, to those in high places in danger of counting these things more than the honor of Christ, — a message to the mere will worker, to the mere talker, a message to the man whose tongue is unbridled, whose character is loose. These things

need emphasis. These things need sometimes the scourge of just such a holy
indignation as we see in the message of
James. There is a time in our own individual life when it would be well for us
to take this message of the old Puritan
spirit as interpreted to us by James, and
read it page by page, line by line, and say
to ourselves, " Does that cut me? Does
that touch my life? Is that a message to
my spirit which I need to give heed to,
that the man of God may be approved,
'thoroughly furnished unto all good
works'?" James has a message, as the
Puritan party has always had a message,
to the Church. The Puritan party has
risen in all the various denominations of
Christendom. There is a Puritan party
that rose in the Lutheran church, a
Puritan party that rose in the church
of England, and a Puritan party in the
Presbyterian church. In England, the
Independents and the Brownists have

been the evangelical life which has
moulded the Church that largely represents the Puritan spirit. It is in the
English democracy to-day you see it;
you read it in its literature, you feel it in
the democracy of England, which has as
its best foundation stone the old Puritan
spirit. This type, broadened, I hope
softened, more purely sanctified, more
rounded by contact with other types of
Christian life, but preserving throughout
something of the manhood and vigor that
marks the type, has yet a great message
to the world. The message to the Church
is very distinct, very pointed. Sometimes
there is criticism. The Church is subject
often to criticism that is captious, that is
a mere excuse for not taking up the
duties of the Church. The Church is
criticised by many who have no intention whatsoever of making any sacrifices
to bring her back to that perfection and
idealism whose lack they complain about.

Such criticism is unreal, unnecessary, and imperfect. But there is also a criticism of ourselves and of the Church which has in it healing, if it comes in the same way as the criticism of James; in other words, if it comes from a heart that represents the hope of the Church, from a love that is intertwined with the life of the Church, and if it comes out of the very yearning for that which is living, and pure, and better than the past. Such criticism is a saving element in the life of the Church; and such critics, far from being cast out of the synagogue, far from having their message or themselves despised, should be hailed as an evidence of the real vitality of the Church, — evidence that God's spirit is still speaking in the conscience of the Church, recalling it to lost duty, pleading with it to take up more fully the duties God would have us do. Such, then, are the criticisms of James. It would be well for us

to weigh at our leisure in detail such
criticisms as we find in the very bold,
very pointed, very startling language of
Puritanism, reproduced all through history, and finding its warrant in this letter
of James. For it has been the spirit of
Puritanism, and one of the notes that
have marked its life, that it has ever been
lifting up and advocating the establishing here on earth of a New Testament
theocracy, to complete the vision, to pre-
pare the way for the coming of our Lord.
Now, we do not share the hopes in every
particular of the Puritans who desired
a theocracy at the time of Cromwell,
because the theocracy that they desired
had very marked limitations, and because we have an instinctive feeling that
any such theocracy would sooner or later,
like the religious society of that time,
prove a failure.   In some way the Jewish
Christian church however, has never lost
hope that it exists to found a theocracy.

The Jewish Christian church fondly
believed that Christ was to come to
Jerusalem, appearing in person to estab-
lish his kingdom ; that all nations would
come up to Jerusalem ; that under the
banner of the Messias come again in
power, the Christian Church might know
itself redeemed through Judah; that, the
regenerated tribes once more restored, the
mission of the Christ would be completed.
I am not sure that Paul did not share
that hope in his early ministry, but, as
you can see from the second letter to the
Corinthians, and from his later writings,
especially the pastoral epistles, that hope
had taken a spiritualized form, just as
the hope of the Church to-day has taken
a spiritualized form, and we no longer
desire to see church and state identified,
doing one for the other the offices of that
theocracy we may have once desired.
But we have lost something indeed; we
have lost much ; and our position, I

think, will have to be taken upon higher ground than we have stood on yet. We should still cherish the hope of the theocracy; we should still hope for such a union of Church and State that the lines will run so parallel that there will be no fear of friction, no fear of hypocrisy, no fear of mere formalism. So long as the State has secular power outside the influences of Christianity, so long we have not as a church done our full duty. We must seek to permeate the State with Christian principles; we must seek to secure the State for Christ; we must make these United States the re-incarnation of the divine spirit. However glorious the stars and stripes may be, however right that we sacrifice our life for our country, we must see to it that the cross of Jesus Christ is still supreme; and the best offering that we can bring will be the stars and stripes baptized from on high, washed from the stains of

past history, that these United States
may be a splendid offering brought to
Jehovah, the seal of the triumph of the
suffering and patience of our Lord, —
such a theocracy as the kingdom that
passed before the vision, not of the old
Puritan of Cromwell's time, but such as
passed before the vision of the inspired
James. He too has a message to the
nations concerning the kingdom ; he too
has somewhat to say of a national righteousness, and of the kingdom that God
is building, to those of you who long for
the righteousness which is of Christ.
Let us feel that that righteousness is to
be a purifying fire ; that in our hearts it
is to burn and burn until our lives are
moulded into the form of the life of Jesus
Christ, as the melted iron is moulded.
Let us feel that love for righteousness, a
burning desire to hold to the cross of our
Saviour, is to be a purifying passion, inspiring us and speaking to us as the voice

of God in conscience, making it impossible for us to swerve from the path of duty, because Jehovah, our God, is ever present with us in all our temptations, strengthening us in the hour of struggle. Is there any one reading this who has not made that surrender? Oh! I beseech you to make surrender of your life to this Christ, unto this passion for righteousness and purity, that you may feel your muscles braced and your hearts stirred within you to seek the higher, the new, the diviner life, the breathings and whisperings of which are now moving amongst the nations. Oh! may God grant that when the time comes for struggles and conflicts, when the time comes for the establishing of the completed theocracy, the inspiration of James may be the inspiration of the Church, that we may lift the cross as the banner of the victory of our God.

VII.

THE MYSTIC TYPE OF CHRISTIANITY.

No man hath beheld God at any time: if we love one another, God abideth in us, and his love is perfected in us: hereby know we that we abide in him, and he in us, because he hath given us of his spirit. — 1 JOHN iv. 12.

IN the formation of primitive Christianity Paul has only one possible rival, and that is John. So far as the intellectual side of Christianity is concerned, Paul stands unrivalled as a formative element and factor. Probably Peter had a more active part in the formation of the external organization of Christianity than the record shows. He probably did much to forward the formation of many churches, without leaving large records of his activity; for it is scarcely credible that Peter should have maintained in the Church's tradition and history the place he has upon so slender a foundation as that which we find recorded in the New Testament. It must have been very largely as an executive, practical man, that he left his mark and imprint upon the Church, which circumstance would explain perchance that it was mainly upon the Roman church that he left this mark. The Roman mind, being practical and executive, would naturally fall readily under the influence of that particular apostle, to whom in God's providence possibly had been committed something of the formation of the government by which the Church was to be strengthened and consolidated. However that may be, Peter is preserved rather in tradition than in record, but John and Paul go down in the records as the two main formative agents in organized Christianity. They were men, however, of very different types. John's

limitations were rather on the side of
that logical, philosophical, and intellectual character which was so pronounced
in Paul. I presume that John, for instance, would have had comparatively
little influence over some of the elements
in the Church's life that Paul has moulded.
Indeed, it appears that in the third and
fourth centuries of the Roman branch of
the Church, John was an almost forgotten
factor. In the Greek church, however,
John takes the place that in the Latin
church has been so largely taken by Paul.
John is to a very large degree the dominant element throughout the Greek theology, which has been so neglected by
Protestant theologians. A great deal of
the disturbance in the theological atmosphere around us now comes from the fact
that there has been a revival of Greek
theology and of the Greek spirit in
Protestantism. We are feeling on all
sides the power and influence of this

Greek revival. Once before the Church
felt the influence of a pagan renaissance
of Greek thought almost absolutely un-
touched by Christian ideas. To-day we
are feeling the influence of the Greek-
Christian thought that has been so deeply
and permanently affected by the spirit of
John. The conception of the Johannean
gospel has opened our eyes to large
realms of truth entirely neglected in the
history of nineteen centuries of Christianity. Once Dr. Hitchcock said, to
the class he was instructing in history,
that the Church had seen Petrine theology
in her organization, and Pauline theology
in her creeds, and now he felt, though he
felt it only dimly, that we were entering
upon a third period of theological struggle, marked by the ascendant influence
of John. He thought the Johannean type
would be dominant only when the treasures buried now in the Johannean writings had become the treasures of the

Church. I think we may look further,
beyond that prophecy even, and hope for
a time when we shall see the Church
doing what the New Testament does,
placing the elements all together, finding for them all their proper provinces,
giving to every type of thought that
has its source in the divine mind its
proper place as a formative element in
the Church's life and organization, and
making the Church the expression of a
national longing for righteousness. If
only we do that, we shall find that we
are united as one spirit existing under
wide diversity. As we have limitations
or capacity, we shall enter more or less
fully into the thought of the entire New
Testament, and James and Peter, and
John and Paul will widen and instruct
us, giving us more glorious conceptions
of the fulness of the revelation which is
in Christ Jesus than has been possible
for us to achieve in our very narrow

conceptions touching the New Testament revelation of God as it is in Christ. We shall see the need of room for wide differences of opinion and statement.

Were we to depend upon John simply, there would be something lacking of the practical Christianity which we saw so pronouncedly in James, and the statements of James are open to serious criticism taken alone. John lays down the law of love. He emphasizes it as it had not been emphasized before in New Testament literature. But if you will read John through, the fourth gospel, and the three letters assuming the Johannean authorship, you will be struck with the thought that there is a class of minds who would find his teaching extremely unpractical. These persons would say to themselves, I have no doubt, " I feel it is true I ought to love my brother, but how am I to love my brother ? How am I to show my love ? " Were we to rely

upon John alone, we should have very
little light upon that question. We shall
have then to turn to James, and find that
he translates into very strong language
the rules and spiritual considerations of
John, and gives voice to the practical
every-day application of the truth which
John saw in such fulness and with such
spiritual clearness. So it is very well for
us that we are not left simply to John for
a conception of that revelation of God in
Jesus Christ. It is a great blessing that
we have John to give us such a spiritual
interpretation of the historic man Christ
Jesus as we cannot find even in Paul,
because Paul knew only the risen Christ,
and such as we cannot find even in the
synoptic gospels, because the writers of
the synoptic gospels were men of limited
horizons in many directions, and of little
comprehension along some lines of what
the real teaching of Jesus was; which we
cannot get in James either, because of

the Judaistic limitations which prevented James from entering into the fulness of the spiritual truth which we find to be in John. John was the beloved disciple. I do not believe that was because of his marked gentleness of character, as some have thought, for we find that John is characterized as the Son of Thunder. He is one also of the impulsive disciples. He it was who would have called down fire from heaven to avenge an insult. He was the beloved disciple surely because he leaned upon Jesus' bosom, because he was able to enter into the thought of Christ and comprehend his mystic sayings. He did not need to have the proverbs unfolded to him as the rather weaker intelligence of the other disciples required they should be. He was one of that inner circle into which Peter was taken, James and John and Peter going with their Master into the presence of the Transfiguration! going

with their Master into the death cham-
ber! sharing the secret counsels of the
Master, who could not unfold his whole
teachings to the dull and somewhat commonplace minds of the other disciples
round about him.

John knew Christ, he felt Christ, he
intuitively leaped to the conclusion even
before Christ finished all his teaching.
He alone was able to give us such con-
versations as that between Nicodemus
and Christ. Mark could hardly have faithfully portrayed that scene. It is doubt-
ful whether Matthew would have understood it much better than Nicodemus,
where we find Christ opening to the
mind of Nicodemus the mysteries of that
spiritual contact between the spirit of
God and the spirit of man which is the
contact of history, of which history is but
the unfolding. It was John that was
able best to enter into the mysteries of
that new birth, which means the regene-

ration and changing of the whole thought
of man about God, and the formation of
that character which is the Divine intent
from the beginning. Who else could
have given us the scene of the woman of
Samaria? And there are often touches
which we should be surprised, I think, to
find in Luke or in Mark or in Matthew,
— touches of spiritual insight, of the
comprehension of the fulness of the gospel of our Lord and Saviour which strikes
us as being unique, and these touches
mark at once the teaching of that apostle
who had entered more than any other
into the spiritual character of our Lord
and Saviour.

And so it is that the picture we have
of Christ from the hand of John deals
mainly with his Jerusalem ministry, because in his Jerusalem ministry Christ unfolded more than at any other time the
real spiritual Messianic kingdom which
he had come to found. It was the Jeru-

salem ministry that most revealed to John
the spiritual thought he unfolds to us.
Christ is for him the divine Messias who
had come to his own and his own received him not; who poured out his soul
in the death agony of the wondrous
prayer which John has given to us as a
priceless treasure in the seventeenth
chapter of his gospel.   I think we should
be surprised to find in Mark or in Matthew or in James such a chapter as the
fourteenth of John; and yet surely without the fourteenth of John there would
be lacking much of the revelation of the
depth of the love of Jesus Christ, and the
assurance that was in him of union with
the Father, which was from the beginning and unto eternity.   " I am in the
Father and the Father in me.   If ye have
seen me, ye have seen the Father.   Why
sayest thou then, Show us the Father?"

Any one who has attentively studied
the language of the fourth gospel will

see at once that there can be little
question as to the genuine character of
the three letters, whatever he may think
of the Apocalypse. They are in the
spirit, nay, they are in the very language
of the fourth gospel. Whoever wrote
the one, wrote the others. In the first
letter of John, we have the emphasis laid
again and again upon that which formed
for John the basis of his religious life, the
enthusiasm of love. What is Christianity? It is impossible for us to define it
in a word. We have to define it as the
contact in and through Christ with God.
We might also define it in its outward
aspect as the new enthusiasm for good
that was brought into the world by the
divine manifestation of the Christ. It is
enthusiasm, the divine enthusiasm of love,
which John makes the basis of his message to all time.

We cannot live for the most part upon
what is known as doctrine, useful as doc-

trine is in its place; we cannot live upon forms and ceremonies, useful as forms and ceremonies may be. We cannot live upon law, although law has its place. If we are to be loving Christians, if we are really to do the work of God, our souls must be stamped with something of the same divine enthusiasm which will burn away within us the dross, which will make us the children of the loving Father, which will send us seeking over the wide world for the service of the Master, that we may be united with him in this divine love, and feel that in love alone can we find union with the Father, that only through love can we know what God is, for God is love.

This is, I think, the real meaning of John's message. His message was an emphasis upon love, — the law of love is the law of life. In one of the Buddhist writings, the Suttas, that especially sets forth the message of Buddha to the learned

Brahmins, there is a wonderful chapter
upon what is known as Universal Love,
and Buddha describes universal love as
being a factor in life which the learning
of the Brahmins had left out. Confucius
dwells upon love as one of the factors of
life. We have in Confucius the Golden
Rule on its negative sides. The Avesta
teaches love as one of the elements out
of which the perfect world is formed and
the absence of which marks the lower
world, which forms the dualism of the
Zend-Avesta system. But nowhere that
I have been able to discover, in Buddhist
literature, or in the writings of Confucius, or in Plato, or anywhere else, is love
laid down as John lays it down, not only
as a law and element in life, but as the
law of life, the very essence of life, the
very being of God, the very evidence of
God to the hearts of men that He really
exists. There is an infidelity which is
the infidelity of a half-truth, an infidelity

that would try to make us believe that
God is something else, that he is sovereignty, or decrees, or law, or judgment,
with love thrown in to temper all these
things. This is the pagan conception,
resulting always in some form of either
intellectual or practical dualism. We
have had many a caricature of God. According to the picture that John has
drawn of him, God is not decree, he is
not sovereignty, he is not law primarily,
he is love, and his very decrees are the
outcome of his love. He is sovereignty
because he has proclaimed the sovereignty of love, and this law of love is
the law of life. This is the message that
is revealed to the Church, the law of love,
the emphasis upon which comes to us
with tremendous and distinct power as
we open the pages of John and find that
he emphasizes only more distinctly and
exclusively that which Paul too recognized as central in his system, which James

too recognized as central for him, which unites the writings of the New Testament into one splendid chorus of praise to Jehovah who sitteth on high, — which is light! which is love! which is God! Walk ye in it.

The second characteristic of John's teaching is the emphasis he places upon what we describe as the intuitive type of Christian character. Paul is reasoning with the Romans and the Jews. He sought to lead the intellects of the Romans and Jews to enter into the secrets of the Most High. For Paul there were many entrances into the mysteries of God's reigning. There was the historical. History was to Paul the steady unfolding of the life of God. Philosophy had meaning for Paul as an entrance into the secrets of the Most High under the guidance of God's spirit. Law had for Paul special meaning as an entrance into the method of the Divine Life. For John

these things may have had theoretically
their place, but for him and for his peculiar
temperament there was practically one
access only. He knew God, — "For I
have beheld him; I have seen him."
He does not need to dwell upon history
or philosophy or law. That might help
others, that was necessary to others, no
doubt; but John had seen Christ; he
needed no other testimony. He had
beheld him. He knew him, not as Paul,
who had a vision, who knew best the
risen Christ, and then had been strengthened throughout the years of his pilgrimage, but because he had sat with him:
" The things which our eyes have beheld, that which we teach, that which we
know and declare unto you to be the
manifestation of God." So he entered at
once without process into the secrets of
the Most High. There must be that
element in all Christian life. I do not
suppose it is equally developed in all of

us. Some of us are sceptical by nature;
if we find God at all it must be through
weary reasoning, walking with tired feet
along the beaten road of controversy.
But those more blessed, those sometimes
whom the world has despised, the mys-
tics, the women in their solitude and in
their suffering, tender children in their
ignorance, and sufferers on beds of pain,
to whom such weary wandering would
be impossible, these have known the
blessedness of entering at once, as John
did, into the life and love of him whom
to see was to know and believe, because
God had given him of his Spirit. God
is love. His love is perfected in us.
" Hereby know we that we abide in him,
and he in us, because he hath given us of
his Spirit." Shall we not sometimes in
the heavenly world, if we are permitted
to reflect upon our past, wonder at some
of the processes that we were pleased to
call intellectual by which we tried to

understand the workings of the divine
mind? All around us, was God and we
knew it not; all around us were oppor-
tunities of love that we never entered into.
All around was the life of God, and because, forsooth, it walked and talked and
spoke as we did, we never knew it!

The early Church had as its spirit that
which the Church in the moments of her
forgetfulness and infidelity has sometimes not fully realized, that Christianity
is a divine inspiration, a divine contact,
— not an inspiration for the apostles only,
not in the New Testament only, not only
in the first three centuries of the Church,
but a divine contact now and always. " I
am with you always, even unto the end of
the world." The question for our consid-
eration is, What is the character of your
inspiration? rather than, What is the
character of the inspiration of the canon-
ical books? We are far more likely to
be unsound and infidel on the question

of the possibility of God's inspiring you
and me to do his work in the world,
than on the question of the possibility
of his having inspired those who have
passed to their rest, and have left the
record of their inspiration as a heritage
to God's children. We need to feel the
power that John felt, the baptism of the
Holy Spirit bringing us into contact
with God the Father of spirits, that we
be no dead memories of the past, but be
living channels of the present, telling
men of the judgment that is round about
us, speaking to men's hearts of the awful
and fearful neglects and dangers of the
present, and the consequences of such
neglects in the past.

John knew him because he had seen
him. We, too, shall be able to make men
see Christ when we too have beheld him,
and have entered into the secret places
of the Most High God through contact
of our spirit with Jesus Christ. We

must be the incarnation of God's living love. We must know God as Love, because he has revealed himself in our spirits, and daily we take up our cross and follow him, becoming like him, seeing him as he is, knowing him, having him dwell in us, and his Spirit to direct us forever and ever more.

This is the message of John; and it is not a past message; it is a message to our hearts to-day. Would you know God? Know him as Love. Would you feel him? Have him in you. Would you live the life that God would have you live, — the life of love? " If any man say, I love God, and hateth his brother, he is a liar. For he that loveth not his brother whom he hath seen, how can he love God, whom he hath not seen?" May God help us to feel the inspiration, to know the baptism, to walk in the love and light that is reflected from the face of Jesus Christ our Master.

VIII.

THE THREE CROSSES ON CALVARY.

*And one of the malefactors which were hanged railed
on him, saying, Art not thou the Christ? save thyself and us. But the other answered, and rebuking
him said, Dost thou not even fear God, seeing thou
art in the same condemnation? And we indeed
justly; for we receive the due reward of our deeds:
but this man hath done nothing amiss. —* LUKE
xxiii. 39–43.

IT was a strange circumstance that
thus linked the life and death of those
two unknown robbers with the life of
one who was to form the centre of history. We do not even know their
names. The traditions about them are
somewhat confused; but we find them
here the victims with Christ of the
cruelty and barbarism of the age in
which they lived. They are called rob-

bers, and no doubt belonged to that class
for which Barrabas stood, half robber,
half rebel against the existing condition
of things, a product of their time, much
as Robin Hood was a product of his
time, much as the bandits of Sicily to-
day are a product of the misgovernment
in that part of the world. For, after all,
character is a strange synthesis of various factors, and it is quite impossible for
us to analyze a character exactly and deal
out to each factor its particular share of
importance. There is heredity of which
we have heard so much, and there is also
a personality of which we are, I have no
doubt, soon to hear quite as much as
once we heard of heredity, as one of the
foremost evolutionists of Germany has
already pointed out that there could be
no progress unless there were new factors
in some way evolved out of the old, for
unless there are some new factors, there
can be no advance over heredity and

environment.   You cannot take out
more than you find in.

We shall be glad to call that creative
factor, personality or will, the element
that gives responsibility, the element
that should sit enthroned, that should
use all circumstances but as a means
to work out the highest in human life.
There are social conditions, environment, and education.   These, too, are
important factors, but if we permit the
will to be enslaved by lust, selfishness,
and other passions, these things become
dominant, and we become slaves to those
that should be but our servants in the
progress of righteousness.

So, no doubt, it would only be the almighty wisdom of God that could separate, in the life of this poor thief hanging
in his misery, the victim of the cruelty of
the time, between the factors that went
to make him the character that he was.
Social suffering and environment had
something to do with it.   No doubt in-

herent tendencies had something to do
with it. No doubt the surrender of his
will had much to do with the melancholy
state in which he finds himself. What
interests us most, however, is to find
what is the effect of this his treatment,
what is the result upon the man of the
measures that society took to prevent
him from being any more a menace to
the safety of the community. We find
that the poor fellow is but the more hardened and injured by the course that is
taken, and the presence of Christ but
seems to stir the ill feelings within him
all the more, and he delights in railing
at his fellow-victim upon the cross. In
the gospel there is no hint of the reason
for the state of mind in which he finds
himself. It must have been some bitter
thought, or some very strange unconscious feeling in him which suggested
his railing cries. He might perhaps say
to himself: " Had I only possessed the

personal magnetism of that leader; had
I only been able to work the miracles
that he claimed to do; if I only had
obtained the ear of the multitude as he
did; had a party in North Galilee been
at my call, — do you think that I would
have submitted to the Roman power as
he has cravenly submitted to it? Do
you think that I would have permitted
myself to fall into the hands of those
who hate me and my people? I at least
bared my sword! I at least haunted the
highways, and so long as my weakness
would let me, I fought the tyranny that
is crushing the Jewish people. I did my
little best to make known that there was
still manhood in Judaism. But this poor
teacher, he claims to be the Christ, the
Saviour, the Messias! If he is the Messias, let him come down from the cross
and save himself and us! But how can
I follow any such craven leadership? I
am glad that the multitudes cried, ' Away
with him!'"

Such a process of thought would no
doubt do much not only to harden the
man's heart, but to blind him to the
high meaning of Christ's death; and
physical agony and defeat and humilia-
tion and shame only deepened and emphasized all that was bad in the man.
His conflicts with society, his outlawry,
his wildly obeyed impulses to disobedi-
ence, these things crowded in upon his
life, and all the worst elements of the
man's character were but intensified by
his suffering.

That cross of Calvary is an example of
unsanctified suffering such as the world
has very often seen since.   There are
those who to-day are suffering, as there
have been those who have suffered all
down history, from the injustice, wrongs,
and barbarism of the time.   This suffering has sometimes been but dimly understood.   Sometimes it has found a voice
in a leadership saying very much the

same things as were on the lips of those
poor sufferers on Calvary. This unsanctified suffering does but harden men's
hearts. There are many to-day just as
bitter as these thieves who rebelled
against Rome! And in all ages there
have been poor criminals who in their
wild despair have wreaked savage vengeance upon those who have thus ignor-
antly and harshly entreated them. We
know very well how easy it is for men to
emphasize all that is wrong in the social
condition round about, how easy and
how natural it is for us to lay upon the
social condition and environment, upon
the things that are external, the blame of
what they and we are. When we are
prosperous and successful in our business
and things go well with us, when everything is very much as we should plan it,
then we pat ourselves upon the back and
say, " See how shrewd and clever a business man I am! What wonderful pro-

fessional success I have! How well I
have dealt with the circumstances of my
life!" But when the adversary overtakes
us, when adversity enters into our soul,
then we look outside ourselves for the
explanation of our misfortunes, because
we cannot bear to divide the responsibility as it ought to be divided between the
things outside and the things within.
And to-day all the factors that have dis-
turbed human history and soaked it in
blood and selfishness are at work in our
land. There is danger of our adopting
to-day merely that which Rome sought
to adopt as a cure for all the evils. To-day
there is danger of lack, or even of entire
absence, of sympathy with those who suffer, with those who are wronged, with
those who feel with fearful bitterness and
passion all their wrongs; and it is an
awful condition of things when these
wrongs are driven home on the one side,
and those who are more or less con-

sciously oppressing the weak are out of
touch with them, and hardening their
hearts have sought to array themselves
against them.

I remember once a passionate, nervous
boy, in ill health, being tormented in
mere play by two or three stronger than
he. I remember the passionate fury and
hate that burnt in that boy's face, a sense
of helplessness and wrong no doubt that
changed everything in him. There was
murder in his heart. It was only weakness that prevented him doing anything
to wreak savage vengeance. At last,
springing at one of those who were his
tormentors, he half drew and half flung
him over the stairs with himself, and they
fell down together. I remember, I shall
never forget it, the white, drawn face of
my comrade as I saw one limb was
doubled under him and he could not
move, and I thought how easily that fall
might have killed him. Then, alas!

when it was too late, remorse came.
Oh! the passions that are roused in
hearts that burn and cry and curse all
the more as their wrong is seen. And
when force meets force, when the conflict
is over and the French Revolution has
done its worst, then superior shrewdness
and force has but to stretch on crueller
crosses the weaker elements they have
wronged.

So history has still the cross of Calvary, still hears the cry of the poor thief
railing in his misery at the helpless victim whom he would at one time gladly,
no doubt, have summoned to his aid if
that aid had been the sword and revenge.
And then there is the other cross, with
the other victim of the same passions and
selfishness of his time. He, too, railed
at first at the Christ in their midst, but
some word of Christ's went to his heart,
or some look of Christ's won his soul,
and he ceased his railing, and even re-

buked his fellow sufferer: "He indeed
without sin, but we justly." He takes
it all to himself, all the bitterness that
might have had some legitimate place as
over against the wrongs he was suffering.
For no crime gives any man a right to
torture his fellow beings as the cross
tortured them.   But he has forgotten
that.   He feels his own sin.   The justice
of the sentence seems to him absolute in
the presence of that which rose over his
soul. " We indeed justly." No doubt
he contrasted in some half-conscious
way the wild scenes of violence upon
the highroads, and the willing submission
of this victim in the midst, and he sur-
renders his soul to the Christ.   There
was no one there to instruct him in the
mysteries of Nicene orthodoxy.   There
was no one there to tell him what the
meaning of the words he had just heard
was.   There was no one there to explain
to him the philosophy of salvation.   He

only knew that here was one to whom
he could surrender his soul: " Lord,
remember me when thou comest into thy
kingdom."

Oh ! what must it have been thus to
share the sufferings of Christ, — thus
to be a help in the last agonies of the
one perfect hero of the world's history ; thus to strengthen the Christ
even by a word when all others mocked
him ; to give the word of cheer and
comfort that this poor robber must have
given him ; thus to give, even in the
midst of his death agony, the last al-
legiance ! Splendid was it, indeed, thus
to share the sufferings of Christ, and
to enter with him at once through the
opened door ! " To-day thou shalt be
with me in Paradise ! " Thus he heard
the Saviour's voice speaking, throwing
open the door of heaven and letting him
in. Oh, what a difference in the sanctified
suffering of this other cross of Calvary !

For any suffering either hardens or
softens. It is one or the other. Either
the rain steals into the earth, watering
the roots and making them glad, or it
beats it harder and harder as it falls; it
is always one or the other. The world's
suffering will do for the masses and for
you one of two things; either it will
harden and drive you away from the real
life, or with broken and contrite hearts
you will find, in the sorrow of the world
and in the tears which you shed, the
entrance into the real life, the life that is
hid in Christ.

Which would you sooner be, Pilate, or
that thief?   Now, with all history behind
you, which would you rather be, the proud
Jewish hierarchy, or that robber whose
very name is unknown?   No justice was
done to him; no doubt the crowd reviled
him as before. Even religious tradition
does not do justice to the poor fellow, for
this is the only gospel that marks the fact

that he turned to Christ. But he had
Christ in his heart, and in the touch of
that unseen hand he had found the
real life that passeth not away, — a peace
which the world could not give, which
the world could not take away even by its
cruellest cross, but which is from everlasting to everlasting.

Then there was the cross that formed
the centre of this picture, with the Christ
praying not for himself only, but for all
of us in the loneliness and bitterness of
apparent defeat. It were something to
defy those who are greater and stronger,
and to die fighting ; but to be hurried
away in the midst of the night, to be
stealthily dealt with, to be crucified before
men could know of it, ah, that was hard !
In the solitude of the cross there was the
shame and agony of defeat, of broken
plans, of purposes thrown aside ; it was
the trial of Christ's faith. " My God ! my
God ! why hast thou forsaken me ? "

We cannot suffer as Christ did in all points, for he was without sin, and we never to all eternity shall forget the sin that we have done. We shall never want to. Some of you have listened to the strains of the Ninth Symphony. The music opens with an impatient struggle with fate, then in calmer melancholy the music grows very simple, very rhythmic, but extremely delicate. Then you notice deeper tones and gradual earnestness, until at last all is caught up and swept together in one last glorious outburst of song. But even then, if you have listened closely, you can still hear the refrain of the minor note that sings to the very last, giving to the whole the earnestness and tenderness that makes it the most perfect of all music.

We shall enter into Paradise with God. We shall know ourselves forgiven, freely forgiven, without condition and without price, — not on the basis of any belief, not on the basis of any opinion, not on

the basis of any surrender. We are forgiven freely; all he asks is that we walk
in the forgiven life, that we feel the
heart of love going out, loving men even
as we have been loved. But even when
we join, as we may join, in the Paradise
of our God, there still will be given to
our song a note of earnestness. We
have been forgiven freely indeed, but our
hearts must go out over the world's
suffering, incarnate in the sign of the
cross. This suffering is our doing, its
cross we must take up daily, but with
the joy of deliverance. It is to this cross
that you and I are to be consecrated.
There is suffering about us. There is
wild despair in the world. There are
awful wrongs. There are fearful iniqui-
ties. How shall we go forward? With
the bayonet? With the sword? With
the cross on which we have drawn and
tortured those that rebel against the
authority which taunts them with weakness, knowing that at last in the ever-

lasting strife superior intelligence and
superior force must ever in the end
crucify the forces of those who seek in
their weakness to throw off the yoke?
Or shall we go with the look of Christ,
with conquering love, even though it
costs pain and toil? For that love
means life, and sanctifying every tear,
every sorrow, brings back to human
hearts the peace that passeth not away, the
joy that comes from suffering if only the
sufferer knows that sympathy is there.
That love lifts men up, adding grace to
grace, and a sweet entrance into the fulness of the everlasting life.   The greatest
wrong is not the cross, the greatest wrong
is the hate and bitterness that made that
poor thief rail at Christ. The greatest
wrong is not oppression, the greatest
wrong is the hate and bitterness that oppression calls forth. The only remedy,
the only thing that will stand between
the two is the cross of self-sacrifice.

This will sanctify your sufferings. To this bring your experience, to this bring your powers, to this consecrate your life, that the Christ in you may look with infinite tenderness even on those who revile the divine, if perchance one among the multitude may turn to him and say, " Lord, remember me when thou comest into thy kingdom," finding in the very prayer a solace, and in the very agony its escape. Or you may crucify the Christ pleading to-day. The historic Christ is beyond our reach, but Christ is with us alway, and you may still crucify and taunt the real indwelling Christ and put him to an open shame ; but he cannot be holden of death. He will rise in power and come in judgment to the life, whether personal or national, and who shall abide in the day of his coming? Lift up your eyes to Christ, share his death, live his righteousness, bear the world's sorrows, and share with Christ the everlasting life !

IX.

THE TEMPORAL KINGDOM.

*The voice of one crying in the wilderness, Make ye
ready the way of the Lord, make his paths straight.
Every valley shall be filled, and every mountain
and hill shall be brought low; and the crooked
shall become straight, and the rough ways smooth;
and all flesh shall see the salvation of God.—*
LUKE iii. 4, 5, 6.

ALL have heard, no doubt, from pulpit
and press unfair criticism of the Jewish
people and the Jewish hope on the
ground that they expected a temporal
kingdom. They had every reason to
expect a temporal kingdom. It was
promised to them. The whole religious
life of the Old Testament was centred
in the State. The prophecies echoed
and re-echoed the hope that Zion should
be the dwelling-place of Jehovah, that

the scattered children of Israel should be
gathered on the mountains of Judea, that
all nations should come up with their
offerings to Jerusalem, that Jehovah
should reign in Zion and the kings of
the earth should see his glory. The
Christian Church would lose much if it
were to brand such a hope as Judaistic
or wrong. We all ought to feel that
there is a glorious hope of a new heaven
and a new earth wherein dwelleth righteousness; we ought all to expect, and
expect with more faith, the consumma-
tion of these prophecies of the Old Testament in the establishing of God's
kingdom on earth, and work with more
energy of faith for it. But I am afraid
that we are just as likely as were the Jews
to fall into the real mistakes that under-
lay their interpretation of the prophecies.
These they interpreted to mean, in the
first place, that the kingdom should be
set up quite apart, and independent of

the ethical demands that Jehovah made
upon the Jewish people. They expected
that kingdom because they were the
chosen people, apart from their responsibility toward Jehovah, apart from his
ethical standard. So even some of those
who had penetrated most into the secrets
of the Old Testament and the thought
of Jehovah interpreted his demands too
much as a form of ritual. They thought
that as long as they worshipped in the
temple, and obeyed the demands of the
ritual and the letter of the law, they were
fulfilling all duty; the temple worship
would indeed be established on the basis
of ritual observance, where the law would
be read daily and interpreted by the
authority of the scribes. They assumed
that a kingdom might be built on things
external.

And they further fell into the mistake
of believing that the kingdom would be
national and exclusive. It would be a

Jewish kingdom as over against the
world. The nations indeed might share
some of the droppings from the sanctu-
ary; some nations might be chosen out
to become Jews and so enter into the
privileges of the Jews; indeed, it might
happen that all nations would at last be
conquered, and in the conquest share the
privileges of this divine kingdom. The
Assyrians, whom the rod of God's anger
broke, and Egypt with her people might
at last worship Jehovah, but the kingdom
would be to the Jews first, and to the
nations afterwards.

Such a kingdom was never contem-
plated in the message of the more spiritual of the Old Testament prophets, nor
would such a kingdom be anything but a
wrong interpretation of Jehovah's law.
The divine kingdom must be, in the first
place, ever bound up in every fibre with
the kingdom of his righteousness. It is,
in fact, to be a kingdom of righteousness,

not of ritual nor of law. Some of the
prophets saw that. " Jehovah is weary
of your sacrifices, your blood offerings;
these things are an offence to him, this
is not what he wants," said they; "the
temple service may be kept in its glory
and beauty, but that will not satisfy the
demands of the heart of Jehovah. He
seeks righteousness. These things are
but a means to righteousness; and as
soon as they cease to be a means toward
righteousness they have no meaning,
nay, they are an offence."

The kingdom of the Jews is only, therefore, for a purpose. The election of the
Jew is only an election to responsibility.
It is a privilege, — all responsibility
ought to be a privilege, — but it is a responsibility that is bound up with the
privileges, and we cannot have the privileges unless we manfully bear the responsibility. Thus as soon as the Jewish
people ceased to be a missionary people,

the Jewish people ceased to be an interpretation of God to the world. They
lost their election, which was to national
responsibility. They themselves knew
that the spirit of prophecy had died
among them. They felt they had no
open vision, and so had no message.
From the older prophets of action to the
later prophets of deed and word there
had been a constant interpretation of
God's word to the world around, but so
soon as prophecy had died, the Jewish
people ceased to have meaning. Now,
unless the spirit of prophecy can be
awakened, unless they recognize that
they were only the mouthpiece of Jehovah, they are to be no longer a people.
When they rejected that which was
offered them, and stoned those that
were sent unto them, then Jehovah
said, "Away with them!" and Jerusalem
perished from the earth; a prophetic
people without a message was absurd.

But the idea of the divine kingdom
did not perish with the Jewish nation.
The idea of a divine kingdom, a God-
kingdom, is the promise of God to all
the nations of the earth, and it is not
lost in the ruins of Jerusalem. It was
revived in the resurrection of Christ;
and we all as Christians are to look forward to the time when all flesh shall *see*
the salvation of God.

"Seeing is believing," the old proverb
says. But Christ says, "Blessed are
they who have not seen, but yet have
believed." There was very gross materialism in the make-up of Thomas when
he needed to put his hands actually upon
the wounds to be convinced that Christ
was risen from the dead. A fine spiritual insight, such as that of Paul in
his later career, would have needed
no such handling of evidence. Christ
resurrected was ever with him; Christ
was in his life. Henceforth he did

not even want to know Christ "after the flesh " if only spiritual vision remained.

" Blessed are they that have not seen, but yet have believed." We look forward to a kingdom. We may never see it, but there is no reason why it should not be real for all that, so real to our life, so real to our hope and to our wish, so real to our feelings and to our hearts, that it becomes a reality in the great life about us. The things of time may pass away, but that kingdom we have seen, and no man can rob us of it. You might go to the poet and tell him there was no beauty, that you had examined all the images he produced in his poetry, you had analyzed them, and had found that they were a strange mixture of the commonplace things round about us; they were not beauty, the beauty was but the imagination, and that it was often in the way of real life. The poet knows better. The artist knows better.

Every man that is touched with the
artist's life, every man to whom the poet
speaks, knows that beauty is a real thing;
that not chemistry nor mathematics has
truths more powerful or lasting than
these realities that give temper to life,
and beauty and glory to the thought
of man.

"All flesh shall see the salvation of
God." For this prophet I suppose that
refers to the terrible time when men shall
be compelled to acknowledge the power
of God against their wills. But we ought
not to be waiting for that time. Should we
wait for the time when we shall be compelled to acknowledge against our wills
that God is not only omnipotent, but that
his kingdom is to be the kingdom of his
Christ? We ought to be so filled with
the faith of the salvation of our God,
so very confident in our hearts that his
kingdom is a reality, and that we are
his children and subjects, that we can

enter now into that kingdom in joy and peace.

What is salvation? What do you mean when you speak of God's salvation? What does the pulpit mean when it comes to you and asks if you will accept salvation? Is it conduct? Some have so defined it. A very thoughtful school of Unitarians in New England, in natural and wholesome reaction against the metaphysical subtilties of a certain doctrinal teaching, said, "Salvation has nothing to do with opinion whatsover. It consists in conduct." But the generalization is as faulty as the one attacked. Salvation is not conduct. Salvation is not character. Salvation results in conduct, results in character. Salvation is no more conduct or character than it is belief. Salvation is not opinion, it is not belief. *It is divine life.* The salvation of God is the touch of the divine spirit with his world that brings into it light

and life, that changes conduct, that
changes habit, that changes opinion, that
changes social organization, that produces
revolution and evolution out of which is
to come the glory and beauty of the second incarnation of Jehovah here on earth.
Salvation is this touch, this precious contact of the soul with Christ, that contact
which sooner or later produces the ef-
fects which that life needs. Look at those
who came in contact with Christ, —
for instance, Nicodemus, the hair-splitting, intelligent, refined Pharisee, won-
dering what this new teaching was that
stirred his heart in some way that the old
teaching had not done. He was hungry,
as many to-day are hungry, for something more than opinions. He went
there to find out what was this new
teaching, and Christ did not give him a
new theology, he did not change his belief, he did not say to him that he must
leave all his old traditions and accept

him as teacher. What he did was to
infuse into the old teaching new life. He
said: " All these old traditions must be
born again in heaven. Into this past
must be breathed the word of God. Into
your life must come new life." How
does it come? I do not know that Christ
ever answered that question, because it
was already answered. Nicodemus had
come to Christ, and in that personal contact and submission to Christ as teacher
had found a salvation which I have no
doubt at last changed his conduct and
belief. But it did not begin with that, it
only ended with that. Take the woman
who came to Christ as he sat weary and
worn by the well in Samaria. The poor
woman seems to have been densely igno-
rant, to have had her mind filled with
the crudest of teaching, the vulgar super-
stitions which had found their greatest
strength, as always, in the sectarian ani-
mosities between them and the Jews.

Christ does not speak to her as he spoke
to the Pharisee. He puts his finger upon
the weak spot in her life, which had been
on a plane she herself knew to be poor
and mean and unholy. Christ gave her
no new ethical code, but contact with
purity, holiness, and peace brings out in
the woman's darkened mind the question
which Christ ever asks and which seems
scarcely answered, because in the personal contact with Christ she found the
answer. " He told me all things whatsoever I did." Here was somebody she
could submit to, here was a healer of her
ethical wounds, here was a purifier; the
woman was saved by contact.

There was Zaccheus, whose life seems
to have been fairly right as to conduct,
but it lacked something. He climbed
into a tree out of mere curiosity, the
world thought, to see Christ. But Christ
knew there was something deeper in his
heart, and he says, " I shall sup with

you," and in that personal contact, Zaccheus finds the thing he needs; a relationship is established between himself and a
spiritual righteousness, and out of this
relationship springs a new conduct, a
changed belief. And out of this relationship and this contact, shall spring a
changed social organization, a changed
life, a new kingdom of God, when all
flesh shall see the salvation of God.

No one of us surely has been without
in his life some personal contact which
has helped and elevated and lifted him
up. We have felt the power of men with
whom we did not agree, men whose intellectual life possibly we felt was far
below our own, men whom in many ways
we could not always admire, but they
had something that we had not, and personal contact with them helped us, gave
us nobler views of life, stirred us to new
thoughts, made us more ambitious for
the future both of ourselves and those

about us. We have felt the power of
personal contact, because we have come
face to face with men whom we admired;
but how with Christ? We cannot come
in contact surely with Christ, for he has
passed away. If only we could walk
with him, if only we could see him, if
only our hands could touch him, that
personal contact would mean for us perchance what it meant to many of the
disciples; but he has passed away, and
with him there has passed a glory from
this earth and forever! No, dear friends,
that contact is possible now and to-day
and forever. It is that personal contact,
that personal relationship, which is the
real spiritual life of the community to-
day. Under all the passing forms of
doctrine and creed the real power is this
personal indwelling life.

Where is Christ? "I am with you
always." Where? "Everywhere." There
is no reason why your life may not come

in contact with Christ if only you will
seek him. He seeks you, if only you will
be sought. Christ is ever willing to make
you *see* his salvation that you may so
walk and never miss it again, never wan-
der again in the mists and darkness which
have sometimes come over your life. I
do not know what you think your life
needs, but it needs everything if you
have not found Christ. It is sometimes
in moments of business depression, sometimes in moments of darkest sorrow that
Christ makes himself most felt, because
Christ came to the lost, he came to the
suffering, he came to the sorry of heart.
It was not to the contented, the self-
righteous, he came, but to those who
needed him. And it is in the moments
when our hearts are bowed down that we
most feel the need of Christ and our
hearts go out to him. When your life is
restless and discontented, when you feel
that your life needs something, some

purpose, some direction, some guidance, it is in such a moment that Christ is nearest to you, reaching out his hand to you and telling you that he will be your teacher, your helper, your guide, he will be to you what you need him to be to you. It may be that your opinions do not need changing. You may have been well brought up. Your opinions may be so far different from your way of life that to change your opinions would not change your life. Then it will not be your opinions that Christ will change first. It may not be your conduct. Your conduct may be outwardly what the world will call moral, what you yourself regard as fairly satisfactory. You may have been able to keep your life fairly clean, fairly pure, but what does it need? If your conduct needs life Christ will give it. On one of the great estates of England the passing traveller is shown an artificial tree, wonderfully painted to imi-

tate the natural branches, but made of
unyielding iron. At a little distance the
eye may be deceived, but only for a little,
and the second impression is one of dis-
appointment and ugliness, for there is no
life there. Far more beautiful are the
little shrubs that grow about the grounds,
that will never reach the stateliness of
the imitation tree, but which have within
them the life that forms anew each
spring the glowing freshness of their
green. What is your morality? Come
to Christ that he may breathe into it the
life that will grow into his beauty, slough-
ing off the old branches that there may
be new life, new glory, new beauty, that
there may be life born of God and quick-
ened by his Spirit.

Where shall you come to him that you
may see him? You do not require to go
to seek him, he is everywhere. Some
have told me where they found Christ.
One in the bow of an ocean steamer,

where he had crawled one stormy night,
having coaxed the sailor to let him stay
there. There, as he looked out into the
darkness of the storm, he found Christ.
It was not in the hush, it was not in the
storm, nor in the still small voice, it was
simply in the touch of that spirit with
spirit. He went back tempted to believe
it was his imagination playing upon him,
but felt as the day went by and night followed day, that Christ had really been
with him in the midst of the stormy
wave. He found Christ, and in contact and touch his life was made new.
Amidst the business of Wall Street,
amidst the tramp of many feet, amidst
the plunging rush after gold and success,
a man walked down that street burdened
with the cares of the world and of life.
Just as he reached the door of the shop
the bell of Trinity struck one, and to his
soul it was the voice of Christ calling
him from shame into a new life, into a

new happiness and a new hope. It may
be in the hush of sacrifice, when we worship together at the feet of Christ, that
you have come in scarcely knowing if
you believe or if you believe not. Christ
was there, loving, pleading, lifting up,
ever saying, " My peace I give unto you.
Not as the world gives, give I unto you.
Let not your hearts be troubled," and in
that touch you have felt the salvation of
our God. And then, if you are true, you
will go out and let that salvation be
seen. Men may not possibly be inter-
ested in your opinions, they will look at
your conduct, they will look at your life.
Your conduct may not bear marked progress at first, but in the spirit in which
you hold your opinions, the spirit in
which you go about your daily duties, in
the new inspiration for righteousness,
holiness, and truth, you will show to the
world around the salvation of our God,—
that Christ is a reality, that he still speaks

to men, that his touch is still felt; and
men will know, even if they do not con-
fess it, that you have something of good,
that life is more than they have made it,
that God is still in his world, is still
teaching men, and "all flesh shall see the
salvation of our God."

Let us avoid one mistake as we try to
make that salvation seen, — the mistake
of the exclusive spirit of infidelity. This
infidelity thinks Jehovah is going to take
out one here and one there from a great
number, and transfer them into his kingdom. That is not election. Election is
not the arbitrary, sovereign act of Jehovah, going here and there and taking out
one to transfer into his kingdom. Election is the choosing in God's sovereign
grace of you and of me to be his instruments in making his salvation seen.
And if we will make our calling and
election sure, then we are to make that
salvation show, — show in business, show

in politics, show in our life, show in our
national life. We are chosen to responsibilities, to contact with Christ, that he
may have contact with the world through
us, — Christ in us speaking to men, telling men that there is a judgment seat,
and a righteousness, that there is an infinite and tender forgiveness, and the
yearning of the All Father for the hearts
of his wandering children. " All we like
sheep have gone astray; we have turned
every one to his own way ; and the Lord
hath laid on him the iniquity of us all."

The kingdom of God is coming
through us if we are faithful; a prophetic, sacrificial, and kingly Church is
yet to rule this world's destiny. The
voice is now crying in the wilderness.
Christ is coming in power, the power of
divine indwelling love. He is to make
all things new. Now, organized Christianity actually obscures for some the
vision of the Christ. Doctrinal discus-

sion, sectarian strife, unholy zeal, are the
mountains to be moved, as well as athe-
ism, materialism, and agnosticism. And
the reign of Christ is to be a personal
reign, for no other kind of reign would
be of any use, just as no other kind of
contact than personal contact is salvation. The Church is to be the Temple
of the living God; its message the voice
of the indwelling Christ.

"All flesh shall see the salvation of
God." Are you trusting in that salvation? Are you making it seen? Do
men feel it in the touch of your hand-
clasp, in the way in which you do your
business, in the way in which you draw
up your contracts, in the way in which
you argue your cases in court, in the way
in which you live in society, in the way in
which you do the little deeds of kindness
that come naturally to your heart? Are
men seeing the salvation of our God, and
attributing it to Christ? Are men seeing

that salvation because they see your life
sweet, lifted up, ennobled, purified, righteous?   Then we do not need to wait for
the coming of Christ; he has come.   He
has come in our hearts, he has come in
his Church.   And when all Christian
men so live, the Church will be a real
incarnation, — the glory and beauty of
his countenance, and "all flesh shall see
the salvation of our God."   God's salvation and the needs of the world are one.
All flesh shall bow at the name of Jesus,
and we shall have no need any more to
say one to another, "Know Jehovah,"
for all shall know him from the least
even unto the greatest.   We shall joy in
our salvation, for "all flesh shall see the
salvation of God," and shall feel forever
and forever the touch of God's infinite
love.   May he grant it!

LAUREL-CROWNED VERSE.

Edited by FRANCIS F. BROWNE.

THE LADY OF THE LAKE. By SIR WALTER SCOTT.

CHILDE HAROLD'S PILGRIMAGE. A Romaunt. By LORD BYRON.

LALLA ROOKH. An Oriental Romance. By THOMAS MOORE.

IDYLLS OF THE KING. By ALFRED, LORD TENNYSON.

PARADISE LOST. By JOHN MILTON.

THE ILIAD OF HOMER. Translated by ALEXANDER POPE. 2 vols.

Each volume is finely printed and bound; 16mo, cloth, gilt tops, price per volume, $1.00.

In half calf or half morocco, per volume, $2.50.

All the volumes of this series are from a specially prepared and corrected text, based upon a careful collation of all the more authentic editions.

————

The special merit of these editions, aside from the graceful form of the books, lies in the editor's reserve. Whenever the author has provided a preface or notes, this apparatus is given, and thus some interesting matter is revived, but the editor himself refrains from loading the books with his own writing. — *The Atlantic Monthly.*

A series noted for their integral worth and typographical beauties. — *Public Ledger, Philadelphia.*

The typography is quite faultless. — *Critic, New York.*

For this series the publishers are entitled to the gratitude of lovers of classical English. — *School Journal, New York.*

————

Sold by all booksellers, or mailed, on receipt of price, by

A. C. McCLURG & CO., PUBLISHERS,
CHICAGO.

LAUREL-CROWNED LETTERS.

BEST LETTERS OF LORD CHESTERFIELD. With an Intro
duction by EDWARD GILPIN JOHNSON.

BEST LETTERS OF LADY MARY WORTLEY MONTAGU
With an Introduction by OCTAVE THANET.

BEST LETTERS OF HORACE WALPOLE. With an Introduction by ANNA B. MCMAHAN.

BEST LETTERS OF MADAME DE SÉVIGNÉ. With an
Introduction by EDWARD PLAYFAIR ANDERSON.

BEST LETTERS OF CHARLES LAMB. With an Introduction
by EDWARD GILPIN JOHNSON.

BEST LETTERS OF PERCY BYSSHE SHELLEY. With an
Introduction by SHIRLEY C. HUGHSON.

BEST LETTERS OF WILLIAM COWPER. With an Introduction by ANNA B. MCMAHAN.

Handsomely printed from new plates, on fine laid paper, 16mo,
cloth, with gilt tops, price per volume, $1.00.

In half calf or half morocco, per volume, $2.50.

Amid the great flood of ephemeral literature that pours from
the press, it is well to be recalled by such publications as the
" Laurel-Crowned Letters " to books that have won an abiding
place in the classical literature of the world. — *The Independent,
New York.*

The " Laurel-Crowned Series " recommends itself to all lovers
of good literature. The selection is beyond criticism, and puts
before the reader the very best literature in most attractive and
convenient form. The size of the volumes, the good paper, the
clear type and the neat binding are certainly worthy of all praise.
Public Opinion, Washington.

These " Laurel-Crowned " volumes are little gems in their
way, and just the books to pick up at odd times and at intervals
of waiting. — *Herald, Chicago.*

Sold by all booksellers, or mailed, on receipt of price, by

A. C. McCLURG & CO., PUBLISHERS,
CHICAGO.

www.ingramcontent.com/pod-product-compliance
Lightning Source LLC
Chambersburg PA
CBHW030843270326
41928CB00007B/1185